# Talk to the Hand

Jose o Isaura Filipe.
Quinta Do Romao.
Lote-5-J4.
8125 Quateira.
Algarve
Portugal.

# Talk to the Hand

The Utter Bloody Rudeness of Everyday Life
(or six good reasons to stay home and bolt the door)

LYNNE TRUSS

PROFILE BOOKS

First published in Great Britain in 2005 by
PROFILE BOOKS LTD
3A Exmouth House
Pine Street
Exmouth Market
London EC1R 0JH
*www.profilebooks.com*

5 7 9 10 8 6

Designed by Geoff Green
Typeset in Quadraat by MacGuru Ltd
info@macguru.org.uk

Printed and bound in Great Britain by
Clays, Bungay, Suffolk

The moral right of the author has been asserted.

A CIP catalogue record for this book is available from the British Library.

ISBN 1 86197 933 9

# Contents

Other people are quite dreadful. The only
possible society is oneself.
*Oscar Wilde*

An apology is a gesture through which an
individual splits himself into two parts: the part
that is guilty of the offence, and the part that
dissociates itself from the delict and affirms a
belief in the offended rule.
*Erving Goffman*

Fuck off, Norway.
*Paul Gascoigne, on being asked if he had a message
for the people of Norway*

# Acknowledgements

As is pretty clear in the text, *Talk to the Hand* owes a heavy debt to two excellent books: Mark Caldwell's *A Short History of Rudeness* and Kate Fox's *Watching the English*. A book about rudeness should start with as many thanks and apologies as possible, so I would like first to thank the many friends who have provided examples, sent me cuttings, or assured me I wasn't barmy not to write the expected follow-up book on grammar: Cate Olson and Nash Robbins, John Robbins, Vybarr Cregan-Reid, Margaret and Bob Cook, Mary Walker, Cathy Stewart, Bruce Holdsworth, Philip Hensher, Faynia Williams, Richard Crane, Gideon Haigh, and Anne Baker. Andrew Hadfield told me the joke about Carnegie Hall. Douglas Kennedy had the experience in the French record shop. To my badminton pals – Andrew, Vybarr, Alan,

Tom, Dan, Vicky, Martin, John, and Caroline – I say sorry (as always). I would also like to thank the nameless people who were quite rude to me during this period. Without them, this book would not have been possible.

*Talk to the Hand* shares only two things with *Eats, Shoots & Leaves*: (1) a title comprising four one-syllable words; and (2) its origins in radio. I would like to thank the BBC Radio 4 commissioning editors who keep allowing me to appear on the airwaves, and in particular Kate McAll, the producer who supervised the original table-thumping rants on which this book is based. "Don't bang the table" being the first law of radio broadcasting, incidentally, I have devised a rather strange method of expressing my feelings in studio, which is to sit at the microphone with arms stretched out to the sides, flapping them slowly up and down in imitation of a giant pterodactyl. Kate has always disguised her alarm at this magnificently.

Continuing the pattern of apology and thanks, I would like to apologise to the many *Telegraph* readers to whose interesting and supportive letters I have not personally replied. I would very much like to

TALK TO THE HAND

apologise – *again* – to the kind stickler from North Carolina who sent me a beautiful wooden semi-colon, hand-carved, and received no thanks until he wrote to check I had received it. And I'd like to thank my publishers and agents: Andrew Franklin, Bill Shinker, Erin Moore, Anthony Goff and George Lucas. Finally, I'd like to thank Miles Kington in the *Independent* for coming up with my logical follow-up title, *Presses, Pants & Flies* (entailing a joke about a laundryman who goes into a bar, does a few press-ups, breathes heavily and then jumps out of the window). I may still use it next time.

## Author's note

The author apologises for the high incidence of the word "Eff" in this book. It is, sadly, unavoidable in a discussion of rudeness in modern life. Variants such as Effing, mother-Effing, and what the Eff? positively litter the text.

If you don't Effing like it, you know what you can Effing do. (That's a joke.)

# Introduction:
# When Push Comes to Shove

If you want a short-cut to an alien culture these days, there is no quicker route than to look at a French phrase book. Not because the language is different, but because the first lesson you will find there usually takes place in a shop.

"Good morning, madam."

"Good morning, sir."

"How may I help you?"

"I would like some tomatoes/eggs/postage stamps please."

"Of course. How many tomatoes/eggs/postage stamps would you like?"

"Seven/five/twelve, thank you."

"That will be six/four/two Euros. Do you have the exact money?"

"I do."

"Thank you, madam."

"Thank you, sir. Good day!"

"Good day!"

Now the amazing thing is, this formal and civil exchange actually represents what happens in French shops. French shopkeepers really say good morning and goodbye; they answer questions; they wrap things ever so nicely; and when it's all over, they wave you off like a near relation. There is none of the dumb, resentful shrugging we English shoppers have become so accustomed to. Imagine an English phrase book for French visitors, based on the same degree of verisimilitude – let's call it "*Dans le magasin*".

"Excuse me, do you work here?"

"What?"

"I said, excuse me, do you work here?"

"Not if I can help it, har, har, har."

"Do you have any tomatoes/eggs/postage stamps?"

"Well, make your mind up, that's my mobile."

This book has quite a modest double aim: first, to mourn, without much mature perspective or academic rigour, the apparent collapse of civility in all areas of our dealings with strangers; then to locate a tiny flame of hope in the rubble and fan it madly with a big hat. Does this project have any value? Well, in many ways, no. None at all. First, it is hardly original or controversial to declare oneself against rudeness. (One is reminded of that famous objection to the "Women Against Rape" campaign: "Are there any women *for* rape?") Secondly, it seems that an enormous amount of good stuff has been written on this subject already, and the plate has been licked pretty clean. Thirdly, and even more discouragingly, as long ago as 1971, the great sociologist Erving Goffman wrote that "concern about public life has heated up far beyond our capacity to throw light on it". So, to sum up: it's not worth saying; it's already been said; and it's impossible to say anything adequate in any case. This is the trouble with doing research.

However, just as my book on punctuation was fundamentally about finding oneself mysteriously at snapping point about something that seemed a tad trivial compared with war, famine, and the imminent overthrow of Western civilisation, so is *Talk to the Hand*. I just want to describe and analyse an automatic eruption of outrage and frustration that can at best cloud an otherwise lovely day, and at worst make you resolve to chuck yourself off the nearest bridge. You are lying in a dentist's chair, for example, waiting quietly for an anaesthetic to "take", and the dental nurse says, next to your left ear, "Anyway, I booked that flight and it had gone up forty quid." At which the dentist says, in your right ear, "No! What, in two hours?" And you say, rather hotly, "Look, I'm not unconscious, you know", and then they don't say anything, but you know they are rolling their eyes at each other, and agreeing that you are certifiable or menopausal, or possibly both.

Whether it's merely a question of advancing years bringing greater intolerance I don't think I shall bother to establish. I will just say that, for my own part, I need hardly defend myself against any knee-jerk "grumpy old woman" accusations, being self-evidently so young and fresh and liberal and everything. It does, however, have to be admitted that the outrage reflex ("Oh, that's so RUDE!") presents itself in most people at just about the same time as their elbow skin starts to give out. Check your own elbow skin. If it snaps back into position after bending, you probably should not be reading this book. If, on the other hand, it just sits there in a puckered fashion, a bit rough and belligerent, then you can probably also name about twenty things, right now, off the top of your head, that drive you nuts: people who chat in the cinema; young people sauntering four-abreast on the pavement; waiters who say, "There you go" as they place your bowl of soup on the table; people not even attempting to lower their voices when they use the "Eff" word. People with young, flexible elbow skin spend less time defining themselves by things they don't like. Warn a young person that "Each man becomes the thing he hates", and he is likely to reply, quite cheerfully, that that's OK, then, since the only thing he really hates is broccoli.

By contrast, I now can't abide many, many things, and am actually always on the look-out for more things to find completely unacceptable. Whenever I hear of someone being "gluten intolerant" or "lactose intolerant", for example, I feel I've been missing out. I want to be gluten intolerant too. I mean, how much longer do we have to put up with that gluten crap? Lactose has had its own way long enough. Yet I still, amazingly, deny a rightward drift in my thinking. I merely ask: isn't it odd, the way many nice, youngish liberal people are beginning secretly to admire the chewing-gum penalties of Singapore? Isn't it odd, the way nice, youngish liberal people, when faced with a teenaged boy skateboarding in Marks & Spencer's, feel a righteous urge to stick out a foot and send him somersaulting into a rack of sensible shoes? I will admit that the mere thought of taking such direct and beautiful vengeance – "There he goes!" – fills me with a profound sort of joy.

! # * !

Why is this not a handbook to good manners? Why will you not find rules about wielding knives and forks, using a mobile phone, and sending thank-you notes? I have several reasons for thinking that the era of the manners book has simply passed. First, what would be the authority of such a book, exactly? Why would anyone pay attention to it? This is an age of lazy moral relativism combined with aggressive social insolence, in which many people have been trained to distrust and reject all categorical answers, and even (I've noticed with alarm) to dispute points of actual law without having the shadow of a leg to stand on. However, this is not to say that manners are off the agenda in today's rude world. Far from it. In fact, what is so interesting about our charming Eff-Off society is that perceived rudeness probably irritates rough, insolent people even more than it peeves polite, deferential ones. As the American writer Mark Caldwell points out in *A Short History of Rudeness* (1999), if you want to observe status-obsessed people who are exquisitely sensitive to slights, don't read an Edith Wharton novel, visit San Quentin. Rudeness is a universal flashpoint. My main concern in writing this book is to work out why, all of a sudden, this is the case.

Another argument against laying down rules of etiquette is that we no longer equate posh behaviour with good behaviour, which is a splendid development, posh people being notoriously cruel to wildlife and apt to chuck bread rolls at each other when excited. Who wants to behave like a posh person? I know I don't. I recently met a very posh person, the husband of (let's say) a theatrical producer, and when I asked if he was himself in (let's say) theatrical producing, he just said, "Oh God, no", and refused to elaborate. Is this good manners? Well, the best you can say about it is that it's very English, which is not the same. As the anthropologist Kate Fox points out in her fascinating *Watching the English* (2004), it is a point of honour in English society to effect all social introductions very, very badly. "One must appear self-conscious, ill-at-ease, stiff, awkward, and above all, embarrassed," she writes. The handshake should be a confusion of half-gestures, apologies, and so on. And as for cheek-kissing, it is an established rule that someone will always have to say, "Oh, are we doing *two*?" Also essential in the introductory process, she says, is that on no account should you volunteer your own name or ask a direct question to establish the identity of the person you are speaking to.

I must admit that this last rule explained quite a lot to me. My standard behaviour at parties is to announce straight away who I am, and then work quite strenuously to ascertain the name and profession of the person I'm speaking to – mainly because I wish to avoid that familiar heart-stopping moment at the end of the evening when the host says, "So what did you make of my old friend the Archbishop of Canterbury, then? Looks good in mufti, doesn't he? You seemed to be telling him off-colour jokes for *hours*." However, it turns out that asking direct questions is socially naff, while the "Oh God, no" response is the one that is actually demanded by the compensatory instincts of good breeding. No wonder I have so often ended up playing Twenty Questions with chaps who seem to pride themselves on being Mister Clam the Mystery Man.

"So. Here we are at Tate Modern," I say. "I'm afraid I didn't catch your name. I expect you are front-page famous which will make this an embarrassing story to tell all my clued-up friends."

"Oh no."

"No?"

"Well, I'm known to a select few, I suppose. Mainly abroad. Nineteen."

"Pardon?"

"You've got nineteen questions left. You've just used one."

"Oh. Oh, I see. All right. Are you in the arts?"

"No, no. Nothing like that. Eighteen."

"Are you animal, vegetable, or mineral, ha ha?"

"Mm. Like everybody, I believe, I'm mainly water. Seventeen."

"I see. Well. Look. Are you the Archbishop of Canterbury?"

"No. Although there have been some notable clerics in the female line. Sixteen."

"Do your bizarre trousers hold any clue to your profession?"

"How very original of you to draw attention to my bizarre trousers. Fifteen."

"Do you own a famous stately home in the north of England?"

"Um, why do you ask?"

"Just a wild stab."

"Well, I like your style, but no. Fourteen."

"I give up. Who are you?"

"Not allowed. Thirteen."

"All right. I was trying to avoid this. If I got someone strong to pin your arms back, where would I find your wallet?"

It's always been this way, apparently, in so-called polite society. People go out and meet other people, but only so that they can come home again without anyone piercing the veil of their anonymity in the period in between. George Mikes made a related point in his wonderful *How to be an Alien* (1946): "The aim of introduction [in England] is to conceal a person's identity. It is very important that you should not pronounce anybody's name in a way that the other party may be able to catch it."

Until recently, of course, people did aspire to posh manners. Hence the immense popularity, in the nineteenth and twentieth centuries, in both Britain and America, of books that satisfied middle-class anxieties and aspirations – and incidentally fuelled snobbery. Books such as Letitia Baldridge's *Complete Guide to the New Manners for the '90s* (referring to the 1890s) or the umpteen editions since 1922 of Emily Post's *Etiquette: The Blue Book of Social Usage* existed because they were needed: as society became more fluid, people found themselves in unfamiliar situations, where there was a danger that they would embarrass themselves by punching the hotel porter for stealing their suitcase, or swigging from a finger-bowl, or using the wrong fork to scratch their noses. Cue the loud, general gasp of well-bred horror. Well, sod all that, quite frankly, and good riddance. Old-fashioned manners books have an implicit message:

"People better than you know how to behave. Just follow these rules and with a bit of good luck your true origins may pass undetected." It is no accident that the word "etiquette" derives from the same source as "ticket". It is no accident, either, that adherence to "manners" has broken down just as money and celebrity have largely replaced birth as the measure of social status.

All of which leaves the etiquette book looking a bit daft. "Wait until the credits are rolling before standing up to leave," I see in one recent guide to polite behaviour. "Don't text when you're with other people," says another. "A thank-you letter is not obligatory, although one can be sent to the Lord Steward of the Royal Household." I experience a great impatient ho-hum in the face of such advice. Once you leave behind such class concerns as how to balance the peas on the back of a fork, all the important rules surely boil down to one: *remember you are with other people; show some consideration.* A whole book telling you to do that would be a bit repetitive. However, I do recommend *Debrett's* for its incidental *Gosford Park* delights. There is, for example, a good, dark little story in the most recent edition about a well-bred country gentleman with suicidal intent who felt it wasn't right to shoot himself before entering his own name in the Game Book. You have to admire such dedication to form. For anyone wishing to follow his example, by the way, he listed himself under "Various".

Manners never were enforceable, in any case. Indeed, for many philosophers, this is regarded as their chief value: that they are voluntary. In 1912, the jurist John Fletcher Moulton claimed in a landmark speech that the greatness of a nation resided not in its obedience to laws, but in its abiding by conventions that were not obligatory. "Obedience to the unenforceable" was the phrase that was picked up by other writers – and it leads us to the most important aspect of manners: their philosophical elusiveness. Is there a clear moral dimension to manners? Can you equate civility and virtue? My own answer would be yes, despite all the famous counter-examples of blood-stained dictators who had exquisite table manners and never used their mobile phone in a crowded train compartment to order mass executions. It seems to me that, just as the loss of punctuation signalled the vast and under-acknowledged problem of illiteracy, so the collapse of manners stands for a vast and under-acknowledged problem of social immorality. Manners are based on an ideal of empathy, of imagining the impact of one's own actions on others. They involve doing something for the sake of other people that is not obligatory and attracts no reward. In the current climate of unrestrained solipsistic and aggressive self-interest, you can equate good manners not only with virtue but with positive heroism.

Philosophers are, of course, divided on all this – but then most of them didn't live in the first years of the twenty-first century. Aristotle said that, if you want to be good, it's not a bad idea to practise (I'm paraphrasing). In the seventeenth century, Thomas Hobbes said that the rights and wrongs of picking your teeth weren't worthy of consideration (I'm paraphrasing again). In the 1760s, Immanuel Kant said that manners could not be reckoned as virtues, because they called for "no large measure of moral determination"; on the other hand, he thought they were a means of developing virtue. In November 2004, however, the philosopher Julian Baggini wrote in *The Guardian*, rather compellingly, that our current alarm at the state of manners derives from our belated understanding that, in rejecting old-fashioned niceties, we have lost a great deal more than we bargained for:

> The problem is that we have failed to distinguish between pure etiquette, which is simply a matter of arbitrary social rules designed mainly to distinguish between insiders and outsiders; and what might grandly be called quotidian ethics: the morality of our small, everyday interactions with other people.

My small, personal reason for not writing a traditional etiquette book is not very laudable, but the phrase "a rod for one's own back" is a bit of a clue to the way I'm thinking. If my experience as Queen of the Apostrophe has taught me anything, it has impressed on me that, were I to adopt "zero tolerance" as my approach to manners, I would never again be able to yawn, belch, or scratch my bottom without someone using it as watertight proof that I know not whereof I speak. Is it worth it? *Zero Tolerance Manners Woman Ignores Person Who Knows Her Shock.* "*She walked straight past me,*" *said wounded friend of 25 years, who was recovering yesterday at home.* "*She is also rubbish at punctuation, if you ask me. You should see her emails.*"

Plus, in all seriousness, there are many etiquette issues on which a zero tolerance position cannot be sensible. Take the everyday thorny problem of modern forms of address. I receive many letters which begin, "Dear Ms/Miss/Lynne Truss", immediately followed by a heartfelt paragraph on the difficulty of addressing women whose marital status is unclear. Well, I sympathise with this difficulty, of course, and I am sorry to be the cause of it. I know there are many people who dislike being addressed without a title, so I appreciate that my correspondents are worthily trying to avoid being rude. However, as it happens, I loathe the whole business of titles, and prefer to do without one wherever possible, considering this a simple solution to an overelaborate problem. True, having ticked "Other" on a number of application forms, I now receive post bizarrely addressed to "Other Lynne Truss", which is a bit unsettling for someone with a rocky sense of identity, but this is still better (in my view) than going along with this outmoded Miss/Ms/Mrs thing. My point is: there is no right and wrong in this situation. Who could possibly legislate?

We all draw the wavy contour line between polite

and rude behaviour in a different place, much as we draw our own line in language usage. That's why we are always so eager to share our experiences of rudeness and feel betrayed if our best friends say, "Ooh, I'm not sure I agree with you there; perhaps you've got this out of proportion." In *Eats, Shoots & Leaves*, I alluded to Kingsley Amis's useful self-exempting system of dividing the world into "berks" and "wankers": berks being those who say, "But language has to change, surely? Why don't we just drop that silly old apostrophe?", and wankers being those who say, "I would have whole-heartedly agreed with you, Ms Truss, if you had not fatally undermined your authority by committing a howler of considerable dimensions quite early in the book, on page 19. I refer, of course, to the phrase 'bow of elfin gold'. Were you to consult *The Letters of J. R. R. Tolkien* (Boston: Houghton Mifflin, 1981), you would find in letter 236 that Professor Tolkien preferred the term 'elven' to 'elfin', but was persuaded by his editors to change it. Also, it was the dwarves who worked with gold, of course; not the elves. Finally, as any student of metallurgy would instantly confirm, gold is not a suitable element from which to fashion a bow, being at once too heavy and too malleable. With all good wishes, enjoyed your book immensely, keep up the good work, your fan."

The idea of the Berk–Wanker system is that each of us feels safe from either imputation, because we have personally arrived at a position that is the fulcrum between the two. You may remember how the BBC always answered criticism years ago: "I think we've got the balance *just about right*." Well, my point is: our attitude to manners is similarly self-defined and self-exonerating. Each of us has got it just about right. If there is something we are particularly good at, such as sending thank-you notes, we are likely to consider the thank-you note the greatest indicator of social virtue, and will be outraged by its breach. In an essay on press freedom in 1908, "Limericks and Counsels of Perfection", G. K. Chesterton saw this subjective rule-making as sufficient reason in itself for not attempting to enforce manners:

> We are justified in enforcing good morals, for they belong to all mankind ... [but] we are not justified in enforcing good manners, for good manners always means *our* manners.

Basically, everyone else has bad manners; we have

occasional bad moments. Everyone else is rude; we are sometimes a bit preoccupied.

! # * !

So, if this book is not a guide to manners, what is it? And what are those six good reasons to stay home and bolt the door? Well, my only concern in this book is to define and analyse six areas in which our dealings with strangers seem to be getting more unpleasant and inhuman, day by day. It seemed to me, as I thought about the problem of rudeness, that it might be useful to break it down. Manners have so many aspects – behavioural, psychological, political, moral – yet we react to rudeness as if it is just one thing. Understanding things sometimes helps to defuse them. Maybe I will save the world from philistinism and yobbery with my six good reasons. Failing that, however, I have the small, related hope that I may at least save myself from going nuts.

## 1 *Was That So Hard to Say?*

"What ever happened to thank you?" we mutter. Ask

anyone about the escalation of rudeness, and their first example is likely to be a quite animated description of how they allowed another car to pass last Wednesday, and received no thanks or acknowledgement; not even an infinitesimal nod accompanied by a briefly extended index finger, which is (curiously) usually good enough for most of us.

What has happened to the rituals of what Goffman called "supportive interchange"? They have gone disastrously awry, that's what. Last year I was a passenger in another woman's car in Denver, Colorado. Waiting at a junction, we received a wave from two young men in a car alongside. I smiled back, and then asked my companion whether the chaps might want something. She opened my window and called across, "Can I help you?" At which the driver of the other car stopped smiling and yelled, "What do you mean, can I help you? I was only being Effing friendly! Why don't you get back to your Cherry Creek Country Club, you rich bitches!" and drove off. Of course, we were both taken aback. My companion, interestingly, was upset most by the insulting accusation of wealth. It annoyed her very much to be called a rich bitch. For my own part, however,

I just kept thinking, "But surely a simple 'No, thank you' would have sufficed? What was wrong with 'No, thank you' in that situation?"

There is a theory of manners that uses the fiscal image of balancing the books, and I consider it a good one to begin with. For every good deed there is a proportionate acknowledgement which precisely repays the giver; in this world of imaginary expenditure and income, the aim is to emerge from each transaction with no one in the red. This involves quite a lot of sophisticated mental micro-calculation and fine moral balancing, so it's small wonder that many people now find that they simply can't be arsed. Nowadays, you open a door for somebody and instead of saying, "Thank you", they just think, "Oh good" and go through it. This can be very annoying if you are standing there expectantly with your pen poised and your manners ledger open at the right page. All you can enter in the credit columns is flower doodles, and these in no way salve your shock and disappointment.

Why are people adhering less to the Ps and Qs? Where does that leave those of us who wince every day at the unspoken "thank you" or the unthought-of "sorry"? Is there a strategy for cancelling the debt? Should we abandon our expectations of reciprocity? And isn't it confusing that our biggest experience of formal politeness comes from the recorded voices on automated switchboards – who patently don't mean it? "We are sorry we cannot connect you at this time," says the voice. But does it sound sorry? No, it doesn't. It is just saying the politeness words in as many different combinations as it can think of. "Please hold. Thank you for holding. We are sorry you are having to hold. We are sorry to say please. Excuse us for saying sorry. We are sorry to say thank you. Sorry, please, thank you. Thank you, sorry, please." An interesting rule applies here, I find: the more polite these messages, the more apoplectic and immoderate you become, as you lose twenty-five minutes from your life that could have been spent, more entertainingly, disinfecting the S-bend. "Thank you for choosing to wait for an adviser," says the voice. "Choose?" you yell back. "I didn't Effing choose this! Don't tell me what I Effing chose!"

## 2 Why am I the One Doing This?

This is quite a new source of irritation, but it goes deep. As I noted in Eats, Shoots & Leaves, good punctuation is analogous to good manners. The writer who neglects spelling and punctuation is quite arrogantly dumping a lot of avoidable work onto the reader, who deserves to be treated with more respect. I remember, some years ago, working alongside a woman who would wearily scribble phone messages on a pad, and then claim afterwards not to be able to read her own handwriting. "What does that say?" she would ask, rather unreasonably, pushing the pad at me. She was quite serious: it wasn't a joke. I would peer at the spidery scrawl, making out occasional words. "Oh, you're a big help," she would say, finally chucking the whole thing at me. "I'm going out for a smoke." This was an unacceptable transfer of effort, in my opinion. I spotted this at the time, and have continued to spot it. In my opinion, there is a lot of it about.

Just as the rise of the internet sealed the doom of grammar, so modern communications technology contributes to the end of manners. Wherever you turn for help, you find yourself on your own.

Say you phone a company to ask a question and are blocked by that Effing automatic switchboard. What happens? Well, suddenly you have quite a lot of work to do. There is an unacceptable transfer of effort. In the past, you would tell an operator, "I'm calling because you've sent my bill to the wrong address three times", and the operator, who (and this is significant) *worked for this company*, would attempt to put you through to the right person. In the age of the automated switchboard, however, we are all co-opted employees of every single company we come into contact with. "Why am I the one doing this?" we ask ourselves, twenty times a day. It is the general wail of modern life, and it can only get worse. "Why not try our self-check-in service?" they say, brightly. "Have you considered on-line banking?" "Ever fancied doing you own dental work?" "DIY funerals: the modern way."

People who object to automated switchboards are generally dismissed as grumpy old technophobes, of course. But to me it seems plain that modern customer relations are just rude, because switchboards manifestly don't attempt to meet you half-way. Manners are about imagination, ultimately. They are about imagining being the other person. These systems force us to navigate ourselves into channels that are plainly for someone else's convenience, not ours. And they then have the nerve, incidentally, to dress this up as a kind of consumer freedom. "Now you can do all this yourself!" is the message. "Take the reins. Run the show. Enjoy the shallow illusion of choice and autonomy. And by the way, don't bother trying to by-pass this system, buddy, because it's a hell of a lot smarter than you are."

This "do-it-yourself" tactic occurs so frequently, in all parts of life, that it has become unremarkable. In all our encounters with businesses and shops, we now half expect to be treated not as customers, but as system trainees who haven't quite got the hang of it yet. "We can't deal with your complaint today because Sharon only comes in on Tuesdays," they say. "Right-oh," you say. "I'll remember that for next time." In a large store, you will be trained in departmental demarcations, so that if you are buying a towel, you have to queue at a different counter – although there is no way you could discover this without queuing at the wrong counter first. Nothing is designed to put the customer's requirements above those of the shop. The other day, in a chemist's on Tottenham Court Road, the pharmacist accidentally short-changed me by £1, and then, with sincere apologies, said I would have to wait until he served his next customer (whenever that might be), because he didn't have a password for the till. While we were discussing the likelihood of another customer ever happening along, another till was opened, a few yards away. I asked if he could get me my change from the other till, and he said, with a look of panic, "Oh no, it has to come from this one." Now, this was not some callow, under-educated youth. This was a trained pharmacist; a chap with a brain. I suggested that he could repay the other till later – and it was as though I had explained the theory of relativity. He was actually excited by such a clever solution, which would never have occurred to him. Lateral thinking on behalf of the customer's convenience simply wasn't part of his job.

### 3  My Bubble, My Rules

This is the issue of "personal space", about which we are growing increasingly touchy. One of the great principles of manners, especially in Britain, is respecting someone else's right to be left alone, unmolested, undisturbed. The sociolinguists P. Brown and S. C. Levinson, in their book *Politeness: Some Universals in Language Usage* (1987), coined the useful term "negative politeness" for this. The British are known to take this principle to extremes, because it chimes with our natural reticence and social awkwardness, and we are therefore simply outraged when other people don't distinguish sufficiently between public and private space. The advent of the mobile phone was a disaster for fans of negative politeness. We are forced to listen, open-mouthed, to other people's intimate conversations, property transactions, business arrangements, and even criminal deals. We dream up revenges, and fantasise about pitching phones out of the window of a moving train. Meanwhile, legislation on smoking in public places has skewed our expectations of negative politeness, so that if a person now lights a cigarette in our presence *anywhere*, we cough and gag and mutter, and furiously fan the air in front of our faces.

There is an episode of *The Simpsons* in which Bart

has a contagious mosquito bite, and is encased in an isolation bubble, and when he is told off for slurping his soup, invokes the memorable constitutional right: "Hey, my bubble, my rules." Increasingly, we are all in our own virtual bubbles when we are out in public, whether we are texting, listening to iPods, reading, or just staring dangerously at other people. Concomitantly, and even more alarmingly, our real private spaces (our homes; even our brains) have become encased in a larger bubble that we can't escape: a communications network which respects no boundaries. Our computers are fair game for other computers to communicate with at all times. Meanwhile, people call us at home to sell us things, whatever the time of day. I had a call recently from a London department store at 8pm to arrange a delivery, and when I objected to the hour, the reply was, "Well, *we're* here until *nine*." There is no escape. In a Miami hotel room last year, I retrieved the message flashing on my phone, and found that it was from a cold caller. I was incensed. Someone in reception was trying to sell me a time share. In my hotel room! No wonder people are becoming so self-important, solipsistic, and rude. It used to be just CIA agents with ear-pieces who walked round with preoccupied, faraway expressions, and consequently regarded all the little people as irrelevant scum. Now, understandably, it's nearly everybody.

## 4 *The Universal Eff-Off Reflex*

It ought to be clear by now that manners fulfil a number of roles in social life. Arguably, their chief role is to make us feel safe in the company of strangers. In his book *The English* (1998) Jeremy Paxman says that manners seem to have been developed by the English "to protect themselves from themselves"; there is an attractive theory that, back in the mists of time, language evolved in humans simply as a less ghastly alternative to picking fleas off each other. We *placate* with good manners, especially when we apologise. Erving Goffman, in his *Relations in Public* (1971), wrote that an apology is a gesture through which an individual splits himself into two parts: the part that is guilty of the offence, and the part that dissociates itself from the crime and says, "I know why this was considered wrong. In fact, I think it's wrong myself." Goffman also explains what is going on when a person tells off a naughty child or dog in public: he is signalling to other people that while he loves the child/dog, he is also responsible for the child/dog, and since he clearly shares the general view of how the child/dog has just behaved, the matter is in hand and everyone can calm down.

Increasingly, it seems, this splitting does not occur – and to those who expect this traditional nod towards shared standards, the new behaviour can be profoundly scary. Point out bad manners to anyone younger than thirty-five, and you risk a lash-back reflex response of shocking disproportion. "Excuse me, I think your child dropped this sweet wrapper." "Why don't you Eff Off, you fat cow," comes the automatic reply. A man on a London bus recently told off a gang of boys, and was set on fire. Another was stabbed to death when he objected to someone throwing food at his girlfriend. How many of us dare to cry, "Get off that skateboard, you hooligan!" in such a moral climate? In the old days, when the splitting occurred, a person would apply a bit of moral honesty to a situation and admit that he deserved to be told off. Not any more. Criticism is treated (and reacted to) as simple aggression. And this is very frightening. As Stephen L. Carter points out in his book *Civility* (1998), people now think that "I have a right to do X" is equal to "I am beyond censure when I do X." The comedian Jack Dee tells the true story of a health visitor friend who was appalled to find a quite large child still suckling from his mother. "I wonder whether we should be putting a stop to this?" she said. At which, the boy detached himself from the breast, told her to Eff Off, and then went back to his dinner.

One hesitates to blame television for all this because that's such an obvious thing to do. But, *come on*. Just because it's obvious doesn't mean it's not true. Popular culture is fully implicated in the all-out plummeting of social standards. Abuse is the currency of all reality shows. People being vulgar and rude to each other in contrived, stressful situations is TV's bread and butter. Meanwhile the encouragement of competitive, material self-interest is virtually its only other theme. The message and content of a vast amount of popular television can be summed up in the words, "And you can Eff right Off, too." No wonder people's aspirations are getting so limited, and their attitude to other people so cavalier. I got in a taxi recently and the driver said, "Do you know what I'd do if I had a lot of money?" I thought, well, take a holiday, buy a smallholding, give it to the Royal Society for the Protection of Birds? He said, "I'd crash the car through the wall of that pub, drive right up to the bar, wind down the window and say, 'Mine's a pint, landlord, and you can Eff Off if you don't like it coz I'm buying the place.'"

## 5  Booing the Judges

The timing was significant. Emerging, bruised and a bit horrified, from encounters with the uppity British public in the 2005 election campaign, the Prime Minister, Tony Blair, launched a campaign for the restoration of "respect". "A bit late," some of us muttered, when we heard. Respect was surely already a huge area for public concern. The humblest lip-reading TV viewer can spot a labio-dental frica-tive (or "F") being formed on the lips of a footballer, with the result that when a permanently livid chap such as Wayne Rooney, with his veins sticking out on his neck, and his jug-ears burning with indigna-tion, hurls seventeen assorted labio-dental fricatives at the referee, there is no interpreting this as, "Actually, it *was* a bit of a dive, sir, but now I've learned my lesson and I shan't be doing it again." Sport is supposed to be character-forming, but people are turning out like Wayne Rooney, and we are in deep trouble. Blaming the parents is an attractive option here, by the way. In 2002, the American research unit Public Agenda published *Aggravating Circumstances: A Status Report on Rudeness in America*, in which only 9 per cent of those questioned thought that children behaved respectfully towards adults, and 71 per cent reported seeing parents at sports events "screaming" at coaches, referees, and players.

Disrespect for older people; disrespect for professional people; disrespect for property – every day we are newly shocked at the prevalence of this kind of rudeness. Egalitarianism was a noble aim, as was enlightened parenting, but both have ploughed up a lot of worms. Authority is largely perceived as a kind of personal insult which must be challenged. On TV competitions, judges are booed and abused for saying, "Look, I'm sorry, he *can't dance!*", because it has become a modern tenet that success should have only a loose connection with merit, and that when "the people" speak, they are incontestably right. Meanwhile, old people are addressed by their first names, teachers are brusquely informed, "That's none of your business!" by small children, judges are abused in court by mouthy teenagers, and it turns out that even if you've got the exact money, you can't buy this jumper because Jason's got the key to the till and he's a muppet, he's out the back at the moment, texting his girlfriend who's just come back from Rhodes which was all right but she wouldn't go again, she's more of a Spain person, if you know what I mean, I like Spain, I've been there twelve times, but then I'm a bit of an iconoclast.

The most extreme form of non-deference, of course, is to be treated as actually absent or invisible. People talk across you on planes, or chat between themselves when they are serving customers. Nothing – *nothing* – makes me more angry than this. I get sarcastic. I wave in people's faces. I say aloud, "I'm sure I'm standing here. Can you see me standing here? Why don't you just catch my eye for a second to acknowledge that I am standing here?" For some time now, I have been carrying a Sooty glove-puppet on shopping expeditions, so that I can at least have a decent conversation when buying stuff in Ryman's. "What's that, Sooty? That will be £3.99? What's that, Sooty? Thank you very much? What's that, Sooty? Goodbye?"

## 6  Someone Else Will Clean It Up

Of all forms of rudeness, the hardest for a lot of people to understand is the offence against *everybody*. The once-prevalent idea that, as individuals, we have a relationship with something bigger than ourselves, or bigger than our immediate circle, has become virtually obsolete. For this reason, many people simply cannot see why they shouldn't chuck their empty burger box out of the car window. They also don't see any reason to abide by traffic laws unless there is a speed camera advertised. "That's so selfish!" is a cry that has no judgemental content for such people, and little other meaning either. Yes, we have come a long way from Benjamin Rush, in 1786, writing, "Let our pupil be taught that he does not belong to himself, but that he is public property." These days, of course, the child is taught to believe quite the opposite: that public property, in the natural way of things, belongs to him.

The interesting thing is that, cut free from any sense of community, we are miserable and lonely as well as rude. This is an age of social autism, in which people just can't see the value of imagining their impact on others, and in which responsibility is always conveniently laid at other people's doors. People are trapped in a kind of blind, brute state of materialism. "There is no such thing as society," Mrs Thatcher said. Well, there certainly isn't now. The latest Keep Britain Tidy campaign has thrown up an interesting moral puzzler for traditionalists by targeting the obvious self-interest of teenage litter-ers. It trades on – well, what else? Oral sex. Ingen-ious, or what? "While you're down there ..." runs the slogan, over the sort of come-and-get-it-big-boy pictures you normally see on little cards in phone booths before they are removed by the police. The idea is that, while you're down there, you will also place empty beer cans in the bins provided.

I have to report that my reaction to the "While you're down there ..." posters is, to say the least, mixed. I am actually revolted by their cynicism, disgusted by the explicitness, concerned that teenage promiscuity might be a high price to pay for less litter, but on the other hand relieved and pleased that, in a poster aimed at young people, the ellipsis has been used correctly and that there is an apostrophe in the "you're". In other words, it actually could have been worse.

## ! # * !

This book is, obviously, a big, systematic moan about modern life. And the expression "Talk to the hand" sort of yokes it all together. "Talk to the hand" specifically alludes to a response of staggering rudeness best known from *The Jerry Springer Show* – "Talk to the hand, coz the face ain't listening", accompanied by an aggressive palm held out at arm's length. I chose it for the title because it's the way I've started to see the world. Nearly sixty years ago, George Orwell wrote in *Nineteen Eighty-Four* that the future was a boot stamping on a human face for ever. I see it as a forest of belligerent and dismissive palms held up to the human face instead. Thank you for choosing to hold for an assistant. There's no one here to help you at this time. Nobody asked you to hold the Effing door open. An error of type 506 has occurred. Please disconnect, check your preferences, then go off and die. Do NOT type PIN until requested. Please continue to hold, your call is important to us. Sharon's in charge of envelopes and she isn't in on Fridays. You need to go to the other till. Have you considered on-line banking? Eff Off, fat cow. If you would like to speak to an assistant, please have your account details ready and call back in 200 years.

People tell me, by the way, that it is possible to get terribly rude service in France, and that I've just had a lot of unusually nice experiences. Ho hum. I also hear from Americans that Britain is friendly and ever so polite, to which I reply, "Surely *America* is friendly and ever so polite (except at immigration)?" and they say, oh no, we're the rudest country on earth. In her book about the English, Kate Fox conducted field experiments, such as bumping into people to see if they would say "Sorry" – which 80 per cent of them duly did. She concluded that manners have not declined, and that when we exclaim at the standards of courtesy on the roads, we ought to remember what it's like to drive in Italy. We still queue up nicely, maintain a belief in fair play, and when we don't like something, we make an ironic joke about it (because we don't like to make a scene). And yet, if you ask people, they will mostly report with vehemence that the world has become a ruder place. They are at breaking point. They feel like blokes in films who just. Can't. Take. Any. More. So what on earth is going on?

# THE FIRST GOOD REASON

## THE FIRST GOOD REASON

---

## Was That So Hard to Say?

The trouble with traditional good manners, as any fool knows, is judging where to draw the line. Politeness is, after all, a ritual of tennis-like exchange and reciprocity, of back-and-forth *pick* and *pock*, and unfortunately there is rarely an umpire on hand to stop play when the tie-break has been going on for four hours already and it's got so dark you can no longer see the net. "Thank you," says one polite person to another. "No, thank YOU," comes the response.

"No, thank YOU."

"No, really, the gratitude is all mine."

"Look, take it, you swine."

"No, please: I insist."

"After you, I said."

"No, please: after YOU."

"Look, I said after you, fatso."

"No, please, after you."

"After YOU."

"After YOU."

Did they ever discover perpetual motion in physics? In manners, it has been around for aeons. In 1966, Evelyn Waugh famously issued a warning to Lady Mosley that, if she wrote to him, she would always receive an answer. "My father spent the last twenty years of his life answering letters," he wrote. "If someone thanked him for a wedding present, he thanked them for thanking him, and there was no end to the exchange but death."

But although it can get out of hand, the principle of civil reciprocity is a solid one, for which reason it is an occasion for total, staggering dismay that it appears to be on its way out. The air hums with unspoken courtesy words, these days. You hold a door open for someone and he just walks through it. You let a car join traffic, and its driver fails to wave. People who want you to move your bag from a seat just stare at you until you move it; or sometimes they sit on it, to make the point more forcibly. As for the demise of "please", you may overhear a child demanding in a supermarket at the top of its voice,

"I want THAT ONE!" Hope briefly flares when the harassed mother bellows back, "You want that one, WHAT?" But you might have known how this would turn out. "I want that one, YOU EFFING BITCH!" shouts the kid in response.

*Please, thank you, excuse me, sorry* – little words, but how much they mean. Last week, a young woman sitting opposite me on a train picked up my discarded *Guardian* and just started reading it, and I realised afterwards that, had I wanted to do something similar, I would have used the maximum of politeness words ("Excuse me, sorry, may I? Thank you") instead of none at all. The near extinction of the word "sorry" is a large subject we will treat elsewhere, but it seems appropriate to repeat here the story of the *Independent*'s Janet Street-Porter, who, while filming a documentary about modern education last year, tried to prompt the children at a school assembly to grasp the importance of apology. "Children," she said, "in every family home, there's a word which people find it really hard to say to each other. It ends in 'y'. Can anyone tell me what it is?" There was a pause while everyone racked their brains, and then someone called out, "Buggery?"

As this book progresses, we will be dealing with sources of true, eye-watering horror and alienation, but the decline of courtesy words seems a good, gentle place to start because the saying of such words appears quite a simple matter. Unfortunately, however, it is not quite as simple as it looks. Besides being the *sine qua non* of good manners, what do these words really do? Well, they are a ritual necessary to life's transactions, and also magic passwords, guaranteed to earn us other people's good opinion and smooth the path to our own desires. Politeness is itself a complicated matter. When it works, does it draw people comfortably together, or does it actually keep them safely apart? And what of its moral content? Surely if we hold doors open, we are acting altruistically? Yet our furious, outraged, jumping-up-and-down reaction when we are not thanked would indicate that we hold doors open principally to procure the reward of a public pat on the back. Why is it so important to us that everyone should affirm a belief in the same codes of behaviour? Why is it so scary when someone doesn't? Should we get out more? Or is going out the problem, and we should actually *stay in*?

Any study of the history of the subject of manners begins with Norbert Elias's pioneering work *The Civilizing Process*, which began life as two volumes, *The History of Manners* and *State Formation and Civilization*, in 1939. It is not, sadly, the easiest of books to read, and I have gone quite pale and cross-eyed in the attempt, but it famously includes a section on the advance of etiquette in the early modern period which has been plundered by historians of society ever since it was first translated into English in the 1960s. Taking such etiquette issues as urinating, nose-blowing and spitting, Elias traces the norms for these activities in western Europe over several hundred years. For example, in the Middle Ages, "Do not spit into the bowl when washing your hands" becomes, by the time of Erasmus' *De civilitate morum puerilium* (*On Good Manners for Boys*) in 1530, "Turn away when spitting, lest your saliva fall on someone ... It is unmannerly to suck back saliva." By 1714, we find in a French manual the excellent advice: don't spit such a great distance that you have to hunt for the saliva to put your foot on it.

Obviously, a modern person is hoping, sooner or later, for the plain injunction, "Look, just stop *spitting!* What is it with all this *spitting?*" – but that's quite a long time coming. For hundreds of years, people were advised that saliva (not phlegm, which is odd) was better out than in, and that placing your foot over your own little pool of spittle marked you out as a toff with finer feelings. What a relief when, at last (in 1774), it becomes the mark of a gent not to spit on the walls or the furniture. Only in 1859, however, does a book called *The Habits of Good Society* flip the whole subject to a modern perspective. You might even say that it overturns expectorations (ho ho). "Spitting is at all times a disgusting habit ... Besides being coarse and atrocious, *it is very bad for the health.*"

Of course, it's no surprise that over a period of hundreds of years standards of behaviour should change and (from the perspective of a modern sensibility) improve. But some less obvious, and very intriguing, points arise from even a cross-eyed and incompetent reading of *The Civilizing Process*, because it's not just about people gradually doing fewer revolting things in public. It deals also with two related shifts: in politics, the inexorable centralising of power; and in society, the flattening and

the civilizing process itself. If one takes the view that modern-day manners are superior to the cheerful spit-and-stamp of olden times, a paradox begins to emerge: while standards have been set ever higher, people have become all the more concerned that standards are actually dropping. Basically, people have been complaining about the state of manners since at least the fifteenth century. The discomfiting behaviour of others is one of humanity's largest preoccupations, and is incidentally the basis of quite a lot of literature. Blame the damn super-ego. If we feel doomed and miserable when we consider the rudeness of our world, we are not the first to feel this way, and we certainly won't be the last.

However, we exist at a particular moment, and there can be no harm in analysing what is happening to manners right now, at the start of the twenty-first century. Theory is all very well, I hear you cry, but I'm still holding this door open and beginning to realise I could die here before anybody thanked me for doing it. So let's just take the holding-the-door example for a moment and see what can be learned from it about the function of courtesy words. Let's imagine that you hold the door open and everything goes to plan: the person says, "Thank you" and you say, "You're welcome" and the whole episode is successfully closed. When that perfect scene unfolds, how do you feel? Well, (1) relieved that they weren't rude, of course. On the personal level, you feel (2) vindicated, (3) validated, and (4) virtuous. On a social or political level, you feel (5) safe. What is quite interesting is that you also feel (6) completely indifferent to the individual who has thanked you, because no personal relationship has been established between you. It is very, very rare for lifelong friendships to be built on a holding-the-door incident. Addresses are not often exchanged. All that happens is that a small obligation is raised, then swiftly cancelled, and normal life is immediately resumed.

So, what happens when the "thank you" does not come? The reverse reactions apply.

1   In place of feeling relieved, you are exasperated – but, crucially, not surprised. Oh no, you are definitely not surprised. "Typical!" you say. As Kate Fox points out, "Typical!" is one of our default modes, along with making jokes instead of complaining, claiming to prefer everything in

moderation, and prizing modesty above all other social gifts. The "Typical!" response is actually quite self-flattering, of course. It suggests that fate can never wrong-foot us because we are always prepared for the worst or most unlikely event. "So then my sister-in-law had a sex change and went off to live in Krakatoa. Typical!" we exclaim. "So then they started bombing Baghdad. Typical!" "The cat turned out to be a reincarnation of a seventh-century Chinese prophet. Typical!"

2  Instead of feeling vindicated, you are dismayed by the rejection of your kindness. Your dignity is wounded. You feel that the world is laughing at you for holding this door open.

3  Far from feeling validated, you feel obliterated. Are you invisible, then? Have you disappeared? Do doors hold themselves open these days? Do I look like a doorman? Would they like to *pay* me as a doorman? (You are bound to wax weakly sarcastic at this point.)

4  Instead of feeling coolly virtuous, you feel a flame of righteous indignation. A good deed has been thrown back in your face! Ha! "Did you see what that woman did? I held the door and she walked

right through! I was doing the *right* thing, and she did the *wrong* thing!" The sensation of being morally superior to everyone else in the world is, of course, secretly the best bit about the whole experience, but beware. What it brings out is not the most attractive aspect of your personality.

5 Instead of feeling safe, you are frightened. You succumb to accelerated moral reasoning. This person has no consideration for others, therefore has no imagination, therefore is a sociopath representative of a world packed with sociopaths. When someone is rude to you, the following logic kicks in: "I have no point of connection with this person ... A person who wouldn't say thank you is also a person who would cut your throat ... Oh my God, society is in meltdown and soon it won't be safe to come out."

6 Finally, you HATE the person who did not say thank you. Indifference is no longer an option. The whole incident has now become intensely personal, although you daren't say anything for fear of reprisal (see chapter four). This person has, through casual and ignorant discourtesy, made you seethe with a mixture of virtuous

affront, fury, and fear – and don't forget, you are STILL holding the door open. No wonder we shout after people, "A thank-you wouldn't kill you!" It's amazing we don't wrench doors from their hinges, run after people, and say, "Here! Open it yourself next time, OK?"

Of course, what we want is for everyone to be as polite as us. The reason I have begun with "please" and "thank you" is that nothing could be simpler than to learn these words. That's what we say to ourselves every day. They are only words! They cost nothing! Also, they are in limitless supply and are miraculously immune to the dangers of over-use. I have recently started playing badminton in the evenings, and last Thursday I managed to say, "Sorry" nearly 500 times in a two-hour period, but here's the marvellous thing: I can still say it any time I want. Obviously, I wish I were as skilful at foot-work and bat-work as I am at apologising – but that's another story. What is so interesting, of course, is that we all apologise to each other; even the really good players. So quite a lot of energy that might be usefully diverted to running and hitting goes into consoling and exonerating, as well. "No, not your fault! That shot was mine! I should have gone for that! You are completely in the clear! You really shouldn't apologise!" Every so often, we try to ban apology from the court, but we can't manage without it. We implode from the effort of swallowing all the "sorry"s. So the soundtrack of our matches goes sorry-sorry-sorry-sorry-SORRY-sorry-SORRY-sorry-sorry, interrupted by the occasional brisk "Yours!" (from my partner) and the responding "Oh no!" (from me), followed by another bout of sorry-sorry-sorry-sorry-sorry.

But the world is changing. Those of us who automatically deal out politeness words in suitable contexts are becoming uncomfortably aware that we earn less credit for it than we used to. It is becoming obvious that we are the exception rather than the rule, and that our beautiful manners fall on stony ground. People who serve the public are becoming impervious to rudeness, either because they are young and don't care, or because they are older and have learned to toughen up or suffer a nervous breakdown. Either way, if you attempt to sympathise with a shop-worker who has just served a rude customer, the response is rarely the one you expect. Mainly you will get a blank shrug, which carries the worrying implication: this person doesn't care whether customers are polite or not. This makes it quite hard to go through the ensuing politeness display without feeling self-conscious, or even quaint. "May I please have it wrapped separately?" you ask, with your smile fading. "Thank you, that's perfect, how kind you are." The ground starts to slip from under you, as no validating response comes your way, yet you are powerless to stop being polite and old-fashioned. "And what a fine morning, forsooth!" you exclaim. "Ha. By God's breath, thou hast a cunning way with yon mechanical abacus! Hast thou a quill-pen prithee? Or mayhap I must digitate upon yon artful keypad?"

At least we are generally spared the enforced perkiness of American service workers, for whom a positive attitude and excessive civility are non-negotiable. Trawling the internet, I discovered an article from 2000 intriguingly titled "The Civility Glut", in which Barbara Ehrenreich paints a grim picture of life under the system of "Have a nice day", "Have a great day", and "Have a really great day". She reveals that Wal-Mart workers are subjected to video-training in the art of "aggressive hospitality" and complains that call-centre workers have started to exclaim, "Perfect!" and "Great!" when she gives them her account number and home address. She has to remind herself not to get too big-headed about how great and perfect her zip code appears to be, in the admiring eyes of others. Meanwhile, she has started to feel embarrassed by her own ritual "Goodbye", because it has begun to sound a bit terse and dismissive in the context of "Have a really wonderful special day with knobs on." What struck me was the example, "I sure don't!", which is evidently the cheerful response you can get if you ask, "Do you have any seats on that flight?" Imagine where this "cruel new locution" could lead. "May I sit here?" "You sure can't!" "Excuse me, officer, is my house still standing?" "It sure isn't!" "Will I ever see you again, my darling?" "You sure won't!" "Doctor, did he leave me one final message?" "He sure didn't!"

However, any effort is better than none. So what is to be done? In terms of making the world go round, these words used to mean a lot. Courtesy words are our most elementary way of indicating that we are aware of the presence of other people, and of the impact we may be having on them. Consideration for others being the foundation of manners, children ought to be taught to use the courtesy words because they thereby learn an important social habit: to remember there are other people in the world. I think it is right to say, "Excuse me" when answering one's phone on the train. I think it is right to say, "Thank you" to the driver when alighting from a bus. We are not invisible to one another. Attention must be paid. The problem, as I hope to explore later, is that people are increasingly unwilling to admit, when they are out in public, that they are not nevertheless – through sheer force of will – actually in private. When they are on trains, or in the street, or in a queue for taxis, they can't say the courtesy words because to do so would explode their idea of the entire experience, which is that they are alone and that nobody else exists. They are, I believe, *afraid* to speak to other people. Hence the astonishing aggression that is unleashed if you challenge them. If you speak to them, you scare them.

However, the magical nature of these words needs to be admitted, too. There is a rather unpleasant aspect to courtesy words which we conveniently overlook because it does not reflect well upon us. As children, we were taught that saying the right words at the right moment had just one function: it was the key to gaining parental approval, which was in turn the key to getting what we wanted. From a moral point of view, this was pretty bad educational practice, but what the hey, people have been doing it for centuries, training children to be crafty hypocrites. In his play *Heartbreak House* (1919) George Bernard Shaw provides the great line: "If you will only take the trouble always to do the perfectly correct thing, and to say the perfectly correct thing, you can do just what you like." None of us can deny that our attitude to courtesy words contains an element of this cynicism. Make the right noises and you get the reward. Deep in our hearts, we recognise that we are merely graduates of successful behavioural training. This does not sit well with our feelings of social virtue. However, the greater happiness gets served under this system, and we can rightly feel proud to be part of that.

Where this magical thinking is now a bit dangerous is in the corollary lesson we learned as children: that if we make the right noises, we may deflate danger, or disarm aggression. Politeness words are not just concerned with making the world friendly and smooth-running: they are an acknowledgement that to negotiate human society we require overt appeasement strategies, such as are adopted by devious chimpanzees in wildlife documentaries. We may draw the line at grooming the alpha male or rolling over on our backs with our tummies in the air, but if we just say sorry at the exact right point, we believe that we may avoid being brained by a screeching savage wielding a bleached thigh-bone.

Politeness is a signal of readiness to meet someone half-way; the question of whether politeness makes society cohere, or keeps other people safely at arm's length, is actually a false opposition. Politeness does both, and that is why it's so frightening to contemplate losing it. Suddenly, the world seems both alien and threatening – and all because someone's mother never taught him to say, "Excuse me" or "Please". There is an old German fable about porcupines who need to huddle together for warmth, but are in danger of hurting each other with their spines. When they find the optimum distance to share each other's warmth without putting each other's eyes out, their state of contrived co-operation is called good manners. Well, those old German fabulists certainly knew a thing or two. When you acknowledge other people politely, the signal goes out, "I'm here. You're there. I'm staying here. You're staying there. Aren't we both glad we sorted that out?" When people don't acknowledge each other politely, the lesson from the porcupine fable is unmistakeable. "Freeze or get stabbed, mate. It's your choice."

! # * !

Two years ago, in Christiansburg, Virginia, a psychology professor came up with a technological solution to the problem of road rage. It was a little green light that could be installed at the back of a car and that could be flashed to say "please", "thank you", and "sorry". I believe a patent is actually in place, which makes me somehow want to burst into tears. This academic's reasoning was that, by means of his "Courteous Communicator", a driver could signal "thank you" (two flashes) or "I'm sorry" (three flashes) after cutting in front of another car.

Naturally, the invention was immediately quashed as unworkable and confusing, not to mention illegal and a bit daft. A spokesman for the American Automobile Association Foundation for Traffic Safety in Washington, DC, pragmatically pointed out that there already existed a courteous communicator in all cars: "It's called a turn signal," he said, "and some people don't even use that."

But how far this chap had missed the point! This nice Virginian man thought there might be a market for his invention – that motorists were crying out for a means of apologising to other road-users and thereby defusing bad feeling. Maybe he imagined it would ultimately lead to an even more sophisticated system of five flashes for "You're welcome" and six flashes for "Nice car, by the way!" and seven flashes for "Hey! You must come to dinner sometime!" and eight flashes for "That would be terrific!" In fact, of course, if he marketed a device for flashing, in orange neon, "Out of my way, asshole!" it would be an instant hit. No, there is one very good reason for not expecting motorists to start, suddenly, interacting with other road-users as if they are present in person. It is that the opposite is happening. When present in person, people are interacting with each other as if they are in cars.

So, one lesson can be drawn from all this courtesy-word malarkey. "Please" and "thank you" may not be so very hard to say, but they perform any number of sophisticated functions that are of no interest whatsoever to a growing number of people. Study the works of Erving Goffman, and you will find exquisite analysis of subtle transaction rituals between people in public – but the main effect will be to make you weep, because his wry observations of "remedial interchange" and "appeasement gestures" are built on the supposition that people are actually aware of each other, and are not concentrating all their attention on their iPods or mobile phones. Blame the conditions of modern life in any combination you prefer. I blame the parents, television, the internet, the mobile phone, the absence of war, the under-valuing of teachers, and I also blame the culture of blame. Richard Layard, in his recent book *Happiness: Lessons from a New Science* (2005), argues that "Our problem today is a lack of common feeling between people – the notion that life is essentially a competitive struggle." Well, that about sums it up. As I mentioned in the introduction, the only context in which you can expect to hear a "please" or "thank you" nowadays is in recorded messages – and hey, guess what, they are not extending courtesy at all, because they are not attempting to meet you half-way. "Please have your account number ready as this will help us do our job more efficiently. Thank you for waiting. I'm sorry you are having to wait." In a world increasingly starved of courtesy words, it's no wonder that when we hear these messages, we want to put back our heads and scream. As Goffman points out so beautifully, traffic cops may ask you politely to get out of the car, but that doesn't mean you have a choice.

# THE SECOND GOOD REASON

# THE SECOND GOOD REASON

---

# Why am I the One Doing This?

I used to write a weekly newspaper column about the internet. This was in the mid-1990s, when newspapers were still in love with the newness of the information super-highway, and had launched special supplements, touchingly unaware that they were playing host to the mortal enemy of print culture, which would ultimately displace newspapers altogether. What an irony. Anyway, my column had no time for this over-excited supping-with-the-devil stuff: it was called "Logged Off" and was mainly a true record of my agonising difficulties just loading the software, dragging icons to the Stuffit Expander ("What the hell is a Stuffit Expander?"), and manfully trying to enjoy the impenetrable humour of computer jokes with punch-lines such as, "Excuse my friend, he's null-terminated." My column included, in its second week, the useful advice: "Things to do while awaiting connection to the internet: (1) Lick finger and clean keys of keyboard; (2) Lick finger and clean mouse; (3) Adjust earwax and stare at wall; (4) Lick finger and clean space bar; (5) Run out of fingers." From this you can deduce what species of fun I was having.

Looking back, it is now clear that my computer's memory was far too small for the stuff I was trying to do, and that the internet was pretty primitive, too. Thus I often waited twenty-five minutes for a website that was crushingly disappointing, mysteriously defunct, or had absolutely nothing on it. Entertainingly, on many occasions the search would reach its eighteenth minute and then just disconnect without explanation. Writing in the column about this disconnection problem, I received many helpful letters from readers, one of which suggested that, if my computer was located at some distance from the telephone socket (it was), I should wrap the phone cable around an item of furniture, ideally a tall bookcase. In my desperation, I tried it. Astonishingly, it worked.

Anyway, the final blow to the column came when,

one week, I had been examining a recommended website about the Titanic and found a rare clickable option, "About the creators". I clicked it, chewed the edge of the desk for the next twenty-five minutes, and then discovered the full, bathetic truth. The creator of this website was a schoolboy in Canberra. He was fourteen. This Titanic site was his science project. I had just spent four hours laboriously accessing the homework of a teenage Australian. It was time for the madness to stop.

When I wrote in the introduction to this book about the unacceptable transfer of effort in modern life, this was the sort of thing I was talking about. In common with many people today, I seem to spend my whole life wrestling resentfully with automated switchboards, waiting resentfully at home all day for deliveries that don't arrive, resentfully joining immense queues in the post office, and generally wondering, resentfully, "Isn't this transaction of mutual benefit to both sides? So why am I not being met half-way here? Why do these people never put themselves in my shoes? Why do I always have to put myself in theirs? *Why am I the one doing this?*"

And I lump the internet into this subject because

it is the supreme example of an impersonal and inflexible system which will provide information if you do all the hard work of searching for it, but crucially (a) doesn't promise anything as a reward for all the effort, (b) will never engage in dialogue, (c) is much, much bigger than you are, and (d) only exists in a virtual kind of way, so never has to apologise. It seems to me that most big businesses and customer service systems these days are either modelling themselves on the internet or have learned far too much from a deep reading of Franz Kafka. Either way, they certainly benefit from the fact that our brains have been pre-softened by our exposure to cyber-space. Our spirits are already half-broken. We have even started to believe that clicking "OK" is an act of free will, while "Quit" and "Retry" represent true philosophical alternatives.

Fuming resentment is the result. You might remember the old *Goon Show* catchphrase, "Foiled again!" Well, we are being foiled again from morning till night, in my opinion; foiled and thwarted and frustrated; and they wonder why so many people are on repeat prescriptions. Everywhere we turn for a bit of help, we are politely instructed in ways we can

navigate a system to find the solution for ourselves
– and I think this is driving us mad. "Do it yourself"
was a refreshing and liberating concept in its day, but
it has now got completely out of hand. In his book
*Grumpy Old Men* (2004), which accompanied the BBC
series, Stuart Prebble memorably refers to the culture
of DIYFS (Do it your Effing self) and I think he is on
to something that extends well beyond the trials of
flat-pack self-assembly furniture. I am now so sensitive on this DIYFS issue that when I see innocent
signs for "Pick Your Own Strawberries" I shout, as I
drive past, "No, I won't bloody pick my own bloody
strawberries! You bloody pick them for me!"

Say a replacement credit card arrives in the post.
"Oh, that's nice," you say, innocently. "I'll just sign it
on the back, scissor the old one, and away I go!" But
close inspection reveals that you must phone up first
to get it authorised. "Okey-dokey!" you cry. You dial
a long number and follow instructions to reach the
card-authorisation department (press one, press one,
press two), then are asked to input the card number
(sixteen digits) then the card expiry date (four digits)
then your date of birth (six digits), then your phone
number (eleven digits), then told to wait. Naturally,

your initial okey-dokeyness has started to wane a bit by this time. You start to wonder whether the card will actually expire before this process is complete. "Please enter card number," comes the instruction. "What? Again?" you ask. But, listening to the menu, there is no button assigned to this reaction ("For *What? Again?* press four"), so off you go again with the sixteen digits and the four digits and then the six digits and the eleven digits, and then you hear the clipped, recorded message, "Sorry. We are unable to process your inquiry. Please call back at another time," and the line goes dead. Unable to believe your ears, you stare at the receiver in your shaking hand. It is at this point, in my experience, that a small cat always comes up behind you and emits a quiet "Miaow" and makes you actually scream and jump up and down with agitation and rage.

But such is modern life. Armies of underpaid call-centre workers have now been recruited and trained, not to help us, but to assure us, ever so politely, that the system simply does not allow us to have what we want, and no, you cannot speak to a supervisor because the system isn't organised that way. We are all slaves to the system, madam; that's just the way it is. *An error of type 3265 has occurred; you're stuffed before you start, basically; click OK to exit; quit or retry, it's your funeral; anything else I can help you with?; thank you for calling, goodbye.* Sometimes I think wistfully of that old TV series *The Prisoner* and how Patrick McGoohan finally blew up the computer by asking it the question "Why?" At the time, I thought it was a bit of a bizarre cop-out, what with the chimp and the space rocket and everything. Now, however, I think the notion of blowing up such an instrument of tyranny by asking it, "Why?" was quite profound. I am always wanting to ask, "Why?" – but stopping myself just in time, because I know the effect would be fatally weakening to my cause. When you ask, "Why?" these days, you instantly lose status. Asking, "Why?" usually signals the end of all meaningful exchange.

So they get away with it, the bastards. Steadily, the companies are shifting more and more effort onto their customers, and even using guilt-trip lines such as "Please have your account details ready, as this will help speed up the process, so that we can deal with more inquiries." The message here is that, yes, you may be waiting for twenty minutes while we make money from your call, but don't waste our time when you eventually get through because this would be rude and inconsiderate to others. "We are busy taking other calls," they say, sometimes. Does this placate you? No, it makes you hop up and down, especially when they suggest you call back later. "We are busy taking other calls. Perhaps you would like to call back later at a time more convenient to us? Half-past two in the morning tends to be quiet. It is a very small matter to set your alarm. Another option is to bugger off and give up; we find that a lot of our clients are choosing this option these days."

I could go on. In fact, I will. So here's a little personal story that still makes me scream. A few months ago, I was in New York (hooray). I had used my Visa card to book some theatre tickets and had then attempted to buy dinner with it. At this point I was told that a block had been put on the card, and that I would have to call customer services back in the UK. I am always okey-dokey-ish at the beginning of these processes; perhaps that is the key to my problem. So I called Barclaycard from my mobile phone, neatly navigated the automated answering service, and finally reached a very pleasant and reasonable woman, who seemed quite sympathetic when I told her what had happened.

Now, I am fully aware that credit-card fraud is an enormous problem for the companies, and that they had every right to check that I wasn't a criminal wielding someone else's cards. However, what the pleasant, reasonable woman said was that, card-fraud being what it is, the card companies now expect customers to make a courtesy call before travelling abroad. I started to hyperventilate. I was about to fly home after spending eight months travelling in America, Canada, Australia, New Zealand, Hong Kong, Singapore, France, Greece and Italy. I had been on forty-four flights. My legs were permanently ribbed from the flight socks. I had seen *DodgeBall* twenty-six times. It was as much as I could do to remember my own name. And now Barclaycard wanted me to clear my itineraries with them before leaving home? I had the brief, familiar sensation that I was going actually insane. "But I don't work for Barclaycard," I protested. "I pay Barclaycard so that it works for me." There was no point pressing the point, however. I had no power in this situation, and we both knew it. I have not ventured abroad since, and I must admit, it's partly out of pique.

My feeling about customer relations in general is that they all adopt this high-handed attitude for one simple reason: *they can*. They are insiders. They are authorised agents of the system. In face-to-face encounters, while one deals every day with nice people in shops and post offices, there is no forgetting the power relation that pertains: as agents of the system, they are in a position to condescend. As mere supplicants, we can petition for attention, but not make demands. Years ago, when I worked in shops, things were different. We deferred to customers because they had the power to spend or withhold money, and therefore controlled the ultimate destiny of our jobs. The old power ratio of shopworker to customer was 40:60. Now it's 80:20, or maybe 100:0.

"Oh no, till's down again," they say, not looking you in the eye, and definitely not apologising, while reaching for a bell switch. "This is always happening to me," they continue, gloomily. And that's it. You are trapped. The bell sounds. Nobody comes. Time passes. Your train departs. A clock ticks. Somewhere in the Arctic Circle, a wall of ice drops into a crystal sea. The assistant plucks at your purchases with a look of mild curiosity and then resumes a prior conversation with a colleague about the final instalment of *Star Wars* and whether it's worth going because the last couple weren't up to much but there's nothing else on, apart from that thing with Orlando Bloom, oh yeah, but Jazza said that was crap, and what about *Batman Begins*, well, that's an idea. Finally, some dim race-memory prompts you to ask, "I suppose you couldn't hurry this along?" But you know the answer in your heart of hearts. "Nah," they say, rolling their eyes. "Till."

Life ebbs away. A tree grows in Brooklyn. Finally, a supervisor comes huffing to the rescue and, without catching your eye, taps a password into the till, and your liberated card is returned to you. No apology, of course. But on the plus side, there is now no need to buy any movie magazines for a while. But shouldn't *somebody* say sorry? Well, the inevitable happens. "Sorry for all that," you say. "No problem," they say, forgivingly.

! # ⋆ !

Now, there is a theory – advanced chiefly by Steven Johnson in his 2005 book *Everything Bad is Good for You* – that interactivity with machines and virtual worlds is making people smart in new and important ways. You were hoping for a bright side and here it is. Evidently, the neurotransmitter called dopamine (associated with craving) responds with high excitement when there is seeking and searching to be done. Johnson is specifically referring to – and defending – the attraction of video games, but I think the science applies also to the mental habits that attach to people who spend a lot of time on the internet or learning unfamiliar systems. "Where our brain wiring is concerned," he writes, "the craving instinct triggers a desire to explore. The [dopamine] system says, in effect, 'Can't find the reward you were promised? Perhaps if you just look a little harder you'll be in luck – it's got to be around here somewhere.'" Games playing may have negligible effects on our morality or understanding of the world, Johnson admits, but it trains the brain wonderfully in decision-making. "Novels may activate our imagination, and music may conjure up powerful emotions, but games force you to decide, to choose, to prioritize."

Now, *Everything Bad is Good for You* is certainly well-argued and important. Impatient old fuddy-duddies such as myself tend not to research the chemistry of neurotransmitters before making sweeping judgements about the harm "interactivity" is having on a generation of people who seem, more than ever, not to know how to interact. Johnson explains, rather elegantly, that old measures of IQ are becoming outmoded because intelligence nowadays is all about application: it is the ability "to take in a complex system and learn its rules on the fly". For young people, this ability is second nature. Any fool knows that, if you need a new and unfamiliar VCR programmed in a hurry, you commandeer any small passing child to do it. But the technology moves on too quickly for some of us to keep up, that's all. Looking back at my "Logged Off" columns, I find that, less than ten years ago, I was working with Eudora and AddMail, and attempting to change search engines from Infoseek to MacWAIS (but MacWAIS demanded a mysterious "key" that I did not have). New email was signalled by a cock-crow, and "No new messages" indicated by an icon of a black snake. I promise you I have no mental picture of this black snake icon. A multitude of techie advances has displaced it.

But enough of this self-pity. Johnson is clearly on to something here. But he seems to be deliberately avoiding a less comforting aspect of all this: that the kind of enhanced brain activity he celebrates not only has a known male gender bias, but is associated with Asperger's syndrome and autism. Confidently defying any such alarmist suggestions, in fact, he argues that, through the miracle of internet connectivity, people are now *more* socialised, not less! It is at this point that I start to make impatient harrumphing and snorting noises. The new social networking applications are "augmenting our people skills", Johnson jaw-droppingly avers. They are "widening our social networks, and creating new possibilities for strangers to share ideas and experiences".

It is true that we are becoming instantly familiar with strangers, and I'll be discussing in chapter five why a lot of older people consider that to be rude rather than liberating. But "widening our social networks"? Well, Johnson is not the first to fall into this little trap of virtuality, of course. Bill Clinton famously said in a State of the Union address that the internet was the new town square. Kate Fox calls it the new garden fence. It isn't, though, is it? It's people sitting on their own, staring straight ahead, tapping keyboards, often in dim light, surrounded by old coffee cups and plates with crumbs on. True, each of us has a virtual social group in our email address book, but the group has no existence beyond us; it is not a "group" at all. True, hot information whizzes around the world with the speed of supersonic gossip, but, crucially, we can choose to ignore it. Many aspects of our screen-bound lives are bad for our social skills simply because we get accustomed to controlling the information that comes in, managing our relationships electronically, deleting stuff that doesn't interest us. We edit the world; we select from menus; we pick and choose; our social "group" focuses on us and disintegrates without us. This makes it rather confusing for us when we step outdoors and discover that other people's behaviour can't be deleted with a simple one-stroke command or dragged to the trash icon. Sitting at screens and clicking buttons is a very bad training for life in the real world.

Also, this god-like privilege of the double-click

is dangerous for a philosophical reason. It blinds us to something significant: that we can pick and choose only *from what is offered*. We have choice, choice, enormous amounts of choice. But that does not amount to free will. In fact, what we do is *select*. We can actively click, and click, and click, but our role is still essentially passive because we have no influence over the list of selections. Years ago, I was asked in the street to answer market-research questions about a new yoghurt lolly. I was asked, "Is it A: creamy, B: fruity, C: refreshing?" When I said it was, if anything, a bit cheesy, the woman looked confused for a moment and then said brightly, "Look, don't worry, I'll put you down as a Don't Know!" Choice from menus is a burden dressed up as a privilege. It is bondage with bells on. And, of course, it still makes us do all the work.

But it is also beguilingly self-aggrandising, which is why we won't call a halt. This is my grand theory of social alienation in the early twenty-first century, by the way, so don't miss it, pay attention. The thing is, we are kings of click-and-buy. We can customise any service. We can publish a blog on the internet. We are always reachable by phone, text or email.

Our iPods store 4,000 of our own personal favourite tracks. Well, sod the gratification of our dopamine neurotransmitters in such an alarming context. The effect of all this limitless self-absorption is to make us isolated, solipsistic, grandiose, exhausted, inconsiderate, and anti-social. In these days of relative affluence, people are persuaded to believe that more choice equals more happiness, and that life should be approached as a kind of happiness expedition to the shops. This attitude is not only paltry and degenerate, but it breeds misery and monsters. And in case you can't hear me thumping the table, that's what I'm doing. Right. Now.

! # * !

Of course, I am not against personal freedom. As a woman from a working-class background, I never stop thanking my lucky stars for the good fortune of my birth; if I had been born even a few decades earlier, my only hope would have been that an obstinate phonetics professor would trip over me in Covent Garden, make a bet with an old colonel that he could pass me off as a duchess, and teach me to stop saying "I'm a good girl, I am." Born in the 1950s, however, I managed without a Professor Higgins – or, indeed, help from anyone at all. I benefited from a combination of post-war prosperity, liberal social change, the 1944 Education Act, equal pay, and the rise of reliable contraception. I used all the freedoms that came my way. The result of all this is that I have, unlike the huge majority of women of my class in history, done more or less what I liked with my life, my body, and my career. I believe in people taking responsibility for their own lives. I believe in being allowed to make choices.

But I really think this has gone too far, this worship of choice. I take my mum out for a cup of coffee and I say, "What would you like?" and I get quite impatient if she says, with surprise, "Um, a cup of coffee?" I want her to specify what size, what type, whipped cream or no whipped cream, choice of sprinkle, type of receptacle, type of milk, type of sugar – not because either of us cares about such stuff, but because I'm expecting all these questions at the counter, and you look daft if you dither. A friend of mine was in America for the first time, ordered a modest breakfast sausage, and was dismayed by the barked question, "Links or patties?" because it appeared to be meaningless. "Can I have a sausage?" she repeated. "Uh-huh," said the waitress, pen hovering above her order pad. "Links or patties?" "Sausage?" she kept saying, pathetically. "Er, sausage?" In Britain at that time, we were unused to there being a choice of sausage type. She had never heard the words "links" or "patties" before. Besides which, in her defence, a patty is surely not a genuine sausage within the meaning of the word.

Meanwhile the choice impulse is being exploited to the utmost degree. "More choice than ever before!" say the advertisers. "Click and find anything in the world!" says the internet. "What people want is more choice," say the politicians. "Eight thousand things to do before you die!" offer the magazines. No wonder we are in a permanent state of agitation, thinking of all the unpicked choices and whether we've missed something. Every day, you get home from the shops with a bag of catfood and bin-liners and realise that, yet again, you failed to have cosmetic surgery, book a cheap weekend in Paris, change your name to something more glamorous, buy the fifth series of *The Sopranos*, divorce your spouse, sell up and move

to Devon, or adopt a child from Guatemala. Personally, I'm worn down by it. And I am sure it isn't good
for us. I mean, did you know there is a website for
people with internet addiction? I will repeat that.
There is a WEBSITE for people with INTERNET
ADDICTION. Meanwhile, a friend of mine once
told me in all seriousness that having children was
definitely "on the shopping list"; another recently
defined her religious beliefs as "pick and mix". The
idea of the world's religions forming a kind of candy
display, down which you are free to wander with a
paper bag and a plastic shovel, struck me as worry-
ingly accurate about the state of confusion and deca-
dence we've reached. Soon they'll have signs outside
the churches. "Forget make-your-own pizza. Come
inside for make-your-own Sermon on the Mount!"
The mystery of voter apathy is explained at a stroke
here, by the way. How can I vote for all the policies of
either the government or the opposition? How can
I give them a "mandate"? I like some of their policies, but I don't like others, and in any case I'd like to
chuck in some mint creams and pineapple chunks. I
insist on my right to mix and match.

Oh well. In his lovely 1997 book *Deeper*, about his

early-adopter adventures on the internet, John Seabrook charts a very different experience from mine
in my days of "Logged Off". For one thing, he got
the hang of the technology a lot more quickly, and
never wrapped his phone cable around a bookcase
on the principle that anything is worth a try. While
I was still bewailing the sound-to-noise ratio of the
internet, he was conducting an email correspon-
dence with Bill Gates. While I was putting my head
through plate glass windows at instructions such as
"You can change the default FTP download directory
by holding down the options menu item, selecting
preferences and changing the directories and applications dialog box", Seabrook was actually being
*flamed*. But he was led to similar questions in the
end.

> When you start out on-line, it seems as though
> politics, ethics and metaphysics ... are reduced to
> their original elements, and are yours to remake
> again ... Why should individuals obey other
> individuals? What are the benefits of individual
> liberty, and what harm does that liberty do society
> as a whole? Why is honesty necessary? What is a
> neighborhood? What is a friend? Who am I?

In the past decade and a half, the world has changed immensely because of the internet, with the virtual colliding with the real. Email, in particular, has had a huge impact on our perception of relative status. For our purposes here, however, the important thing is that all the clicking and searching may appear to be an active pursuit of knowledge, but it is still hard work with no guarantee of reward in the context of cold impersonality. Two and a half millennia of Socratic educational practice have been swept aside in fifteen years. The message now is, if you want knowledge, go and find it, good luck, sit there, don't move, see you later. And make friends with your dopamine. You won't get anywhere without it.

Doesn't the same alienating, laborious impotence mark our everyday dealings with the people who ought to be serving us? We make all the effort, just to find out how far we can get, and sometimes it isn't very far. The individual is now virtually brainwashed into accepting that clicking menus, punching buttons, and self-channelling are the nearest you can get to asking a question. "Why am I the one doing this? Shouldn't they be meeting me half-way?

Isn't this *rude?*" we cry – but we will probably be the last ones to see things this way. And now I must get on with calling Barclaycard. I am thinking of taking a trip, and I need to make sure they will let me.

# THE THIRD GOOD REASON

# THE THIRD GOOD REASON

## My Bubble, My Rules

In October 2004, a fifteen-year-old girl at a school near Swindon became the centre of a news story when she spearheaded a rebellion. Apparently, the school's head teacher had "reminded" pupils that they were not allowed to hold hands, kiss, or otherwise parade their sexuality in "the workplace". Outraged, the pupils fought back. They staged a 200-strong strike plus a rally, and then set about petitioning the governors. This was an infringement of their human rights! "At sixteen, you can get married," argued the fifteen-year-old who got herself into the papers. "So to say you're not allowed to touch each other is ridiculous."

In February 2005, the Virginia State House of Representatives voted by a 60–34 majority to outlaw the wearing of low-slung jeans. The so-called

Droopy-Drawer Bill forbade the exposure of underwear in a way that was "lewd or indecent". The bill's sponsor told the house: "To vote for this bill would be a vote for character, to uplift your community and to do something good not only for the state of Virginia, but for this entire country." "Underwear is called underwear for a reason," commented one of his colleagues.

In June 2005, the London *Evening Standard* broke the news we had all been waiting for: "Soon We'll Watch TV As We Travel on the Tube." Evidently a trial of the new service will begin in 2006, and full service should be in place by the following year. "London Underground is planning to install the necessary technology to access broadcasts via the phone and digital radio. It also plans to offer wireless internet access in stations and on trains so that commuters using laptops can check their email or surf the net." Might there be "quiet" carriages, where people could escape the TV, radio, phoning, and surfing? No. "We will focus on education instead," said a spokesman. "People need to be told to be tolerant, so we will be running ads similar to those found on overground trains."

In March 2005, the *New York Times* ran a story headlined "No Need to Stew: A Few Tips to Cope with Life's Annoyances", about people who were taking small revenges on the annoyances of modern life. One Mr Williams (of Melrose, NY) had devised a way of settling the score against junk-mailers, which entailed inserting heavy paper and small strips of sheet metal in the business-reply envelopes, thus forcing the junk-mailers to pay huge extra postage. "You wouldn't believe how heavy I got some of those envelopes to weigh," he said. A spokesman for the United States Postal Service said that Mr Williams's actions sounded legal, as long as the envelope was properly sealed.

In papers everywhere for the past year or two, there has been larky but desperate advice from columnists and stand-up comedians on how to deal with cold callers, either on the phone or in person. First prize goes to the *Independent*'s Charles Nevin, who came up with: "Thank goodness! Do you have experience in restraining people?" as a way of dealing with nuisance callers on the doorstep. Close runner-up was his colleague Deborah Ross, who described how her partner always asks flatly, "Are you selling something?" When this is hastily denied, he says, "That's a pity. I was in the mood for buying something over the phone, whatever the cost. But now I fear the moment has passed. Goodbye."

Finally, in *The Guardian* in April 2005, came the story of research conducted by a psychiatrist from King's College London, which proved that the distractions of constant emails, text and phone messages were a greater threat to concentration and IQ than smoking cannabis. "Respondents' minds were all over the place as they faced new questions and challenges every time an email dropped into their inbox," wrote Martin Wainwright. "Manners are also going by the board, with one in five of the respondents breaking off from meals or social engagements to receive and deal with messages. Although nine out of ten agreed that answering messages during face-to-face meetings or office conferences was rude, a third nonetheless felt that this had become 'acceptable and seen as a sign of diligence and efficiency'."

! # * !

Sometimes I think we were better off before the term "personal space" escaped from sociology and got mixed up with popular ideas of entitlement. It is now, however, firmly in the *Oxford Dictionary of English*, defined as "The physical space immediately surrounding someone, into which encroachment can feel uncomfortable or threatening." You will note that there is no measurement indicated in this definition, such as "Generally accepted to be about a yard behind and two yards in front", which is an oversight on the part of the ODE, I think, because a lot of people would like to know their precise rights where personal space is concerned. As it is, everyone is tiresomely free to define their personal space subjectively, and to appeal to it when it suits them. Rude people are especially fond of the personal-space defence. Children insist on their right to personal space. Even my cat knows about it. You should see the way he looks at me when I attempt to share the comfy chair with him in front of the telly. "Budge up," I say, cheerfully. "The golf's on. You don't even like golf. Name me one player you recognise." And he purses his lips in that peculiar long-suffering, affronted-cat way, and I can hear him thinking, "I don't believe it. She's invading my personal space *again*."

I have to admit, I am rather keen on keeping other people at arm's length. If a chap stands an inch behind me and loudly crunches and slurps an apple, I suffer and moan and clench all the clench-able parts of my anatomy, but what I really want to do (please don't tell anybody) is to turn round on the spot with fists raised, and with an efficient, clean one-two, knock all his teeth out. What I would really appreciate is a kind of negative polarity I could switch on in personal-space emergencies; in fact, now I think of it, is there any lovelier, more com-forting four-word combination than "Activate the force field"? All my life, I seem to have seen won-derful, battery-draining force fields demonstrated in science-fiction movies, but let me tell you: if you try to buy one, you draw a blank. You can't even get an automatic apple-atomiser that will detect inappro-priately propinquitous apple-consumption, blow the fruit to smithereens and deliver a mild inciden-tal electric shock to the genitals. No, personal space is still an ideal rather than a solid reality off which bullets would bounce and swords glance. The best mental picture I can come up with for personal space as we know it is a spherical membrane eight feet in diameter with a person inside it, bowling along like a hamster in a ball.

All the news stories above – about the Swindon schoolgirl, the man sending sheet metal through the post, and so on – are concerned with the notion of "space", one way or another. The trouble is, our own personal space always seems to be up for grabs in unacceptable ways. Other people don't respect our personal space and are conducting private phone conversations in public places, regardless of the annoyance they cause. Which is very, very rude of them. Ask people about rudeness, and after "Why don't people say thank you?" and "Why am I always the one doing everything?", the subject of annoying mobile phone users comes up more quickly than you can say "I'm on the train." What is happening? Why is this such a big issue? Have some people truly lost all sense of being out in public? Has some vital inhibitor in their brains been switched off? Surely we all agree that the question "Should I do this?" ought to have an automatic subsidiary question, "Should I do this *here*?" But on the other hand, are some of us extending our personal space an unreasonable distance – basically, for as far as the eye can see or the ear can hear? Why don't we accept that being out of doors means being with other people who do things we can't control?

In reality, mostly people on public transport listen inoffensively to iPods, or quietly text on their mobile phones, which are private activities designed simply to remove them from their surroundings, in pretty much the same way that reading a newspaper both passes the time and sends out the barrier signal, "Leave me alone." Yet there is something more profound going on. Our hamster balls just keep clashing with other people's hamster balls, and it isn't comfortable. The fifteen-year-old Swindon girl feels she has a right to canoodle at school. Academic friends say their students answer calls during lectures. Lovers lolling on the public grass on a sunny day glare at you if you look at them, as if you have just walked into their living-room. People chat in the cinema during the film, and sometimes in the theatre during the play. Air travellers on long-haul flights change into pyjamas in the lavatories. It's as if we now believe, in some spooky virtual way, that wherever we are, it's home.

! # * !

I have a rather heretical view when it comes to mobile phones, so I'd better confess to it at once. I don't mind people saying, "I'm on the train." It truly doesn't annoy me. Here are the things that drive me nuts when I'm out. I can't stand people talking in the cinema. I can't stand other people's cigarette smoke, especially outdoors. I am scared and angry when I hear the approach of young men drunkenly shouting. I can't stand children skateboarding on pavements, or cyclists jumping lights and performing speed slaloms between pedestrians, and I am offended by T-shirts with ugly Eff-Off messages on them. It was, however, the rather mild "Bored of the Beckhams" that was my least favourite T-shirt slogan of recent years, for the usual shameful pedantic reasons. "Bored *with* the Beckhams!" I would inwardly moan, reaching for the smelling salts in my lavender portmanteau. "Or even bored *by* the Beckhams, if you must! But bored *of* the Beckhams? Never, my dear, *never!*"

What else? Well, I am incensed by graffiti, and would like to see offenders sprayed all over with car-paint and then strung up for public humiliation. (As you can tell, I've given a lot of thought to that one.) I also can't abide to see people drop litter; it truly shocks me. People of all ages evidently think nothing of reaching into a bag, discovering something surplus to requirements, holding it out at arm's length and then insouciantly *letting go*. Walking along the Brighton seafront one balmy evening, I saw a woman perform a nappy-change on a public bench and then just leave the old nappy and the paper towels behind, when there was a litter-bin about fifteen feet away. Occasionally I will confront a litter-bug, running after them and saying, "Excuse me, I think you dropped this." But, well, I say "occasionally"; I've done it twice. Sensibly I weigh the odds. If the person is bigger than me, or is (very important consideration, this) *accompanied by* anyone bigger than me, I walk away. As a litter-bug vigilante, I know my limits. If they are over five foot two, or older than four, I let it go.

But as I say, the thing that doesn't drive me nuts is other people's mobile phones – mainly, I suspect, because I have one myself, but also because hearing a stranger on the phone humanises them in (to me) a generally welcome way, whereas watching them blow smoke in the air or drop soiled tissue or deface a building does quite the opposite. It seems to me obvious that "I'm on the train" is the main thing you will hear other people say, because – being reasonable about it – the train is the main place you are likely to hear people talking on mobile phones. If they said instead, "I'm in the bath" you'd think, hang on, no you're not, you're on the train. Actually, the only depressing aspect of this is how boringly honest people are. They seem to have no imagination at all. When they say, "Just pulling into Haywards Heath, dear," I look up optimistically every time, but dammit, we always are just pulling into Haywards Heath. I yearn to hear someone say, "Yes, dear; next stop Albuquerque", when the train is arriving in Ramsgate. "Yes, the dog's with me, he sends a woof, don't you, boy, eh, yes you do, yes you do (ruff, ruff!)" when there's actually no dog anywhere in sight.

To me, the delight of people answering or making calls is that they suddenly – and oblivious to the enforced eavesdropping – reveal enormous amounts about themselves, as if they had, under the influence of hypnosis, stood up on a table and started stripping, and then, just as suddenly, got down again, adjusted their clothing, and resumed the anonymity of the everyday humdrum passenger. Of course, I have overheard – and resented – banal, annoying, and even obscene mobile calls. A friend of mine travelling from Victoria to Brighton was obliged to overhear all the arrangements for the felonious handover of counterfeit money ("That last lot was like bog paper!" the bloke yelled, striking terror in all his fellow passengers). I once stood in misery in a taxi queue while a huge drunk man behind me bellowed a rather vile account of the evening's sexual exploits ("I said to her, 'No nails, love! No nails! The wife'll Effing kill me!'"). But on the whole, I rather welcome the chance it gives us to overhear other people's business. And of course one day I'll hear someone standing outside Waterloo station saying, "Yes, Istanbul is so magical in the springtime!" and it will make me very happy.

But just because I find it quite interesting doesn't mean that it isn't yet another symptom of our almost insane levels of self-absorption. The trouble is, the telephone has always had the ability to distract us from our duty to our surroundings; it is, quite simply, an anti-social instrument. When you are talking to someone face-to-face and the phone interrupts you, you can be as polite as you like about it ("Excuse me, do you mind, I'm sorry"), but it's still a snub to the person present. I used to visit a friend in her office, and would often go through a very painful pantomime when she answered the phone, because she would launch into an animated conversation immediately, but when I mimed a discreet "I'll go, then", she would wave and frown at me, insisting I stay, and roll her eyes exaggeratedly at how annoying it was to be on the phone to this total bore, all the while laughing and chatting, and giving no verbal indication that she had someone present in her office and therefore ought to cut it short. "And *then what*?" she would ask, beckoning me back as I tried to escape. "No! Really? I've always thought that about him!" I would writhe in agony at how rude she was being to me, how rude she was being to the other person (who didn't know), and how miserable I was, having to listen to all this. Imagine calling her up, after witnessing scenes like this. "Is this a bad moment?" I would ask. "Is there anyone there? Who's there? I bet there's someone there!" "No, of course there isn't!" she would assure me, but I still imagined her scribbling my name on a piece of paper, pushing it across the desk, and miming being sick down a lavatory.

When people look for a piece of technology to blame for modern manners, it is often television that cops the lot, but we forget what an impact the telephone had when it was first introduced. With the advent of the phone, people could choose to conduct real-time private conversations with people *who weren't there*. Having grown up with universal telephone technology, we find this idea pretty unremarkable, but Carolyn Marvin's fascinating book *When Old Technologies were New* (1988) points out that there were considerable fears in the last quarter of the nineteenth century about the impact the telephone would have – quite common-sense fears, actually, that mainly came true, and that neatly parallel our current concerns about the internet. The telephone was an instrument for speaking to someone who couldn't see you, and who could be many miles away. It cut through normal social etiquette. Because of these factors, it would make people more confiding and open, but also less civil, less deferential, and less honest. It would facilitate crime. Children would become furtive, anti-social, and uncontrollable. Young people could make assignations with it. None of this seems ridiculous or alarmist to me, incidentally, except perhaps for the warning from the editor of a Philadelphia newspaper in 1894 who cautioned his readers "not to converse by phone with ill persons for fear of contracting contagious diseases".

The impact of the phone on the "proprieties of presence" was immediately worrying. People spoke more freely on the telephone. Women gossiped on it. Formerly, there was a code for speaking when at home, and a code for speaking when outside the home. Both codes were posited on observing the presence of others and the etiquette of the surroundings. But the phone was one-to-one, and neither indoors nor outdoors, and the four walls of domestic privacy were breached for ever. "The home wears a vanishing aspect," lamented *Harper's* in 1893. Carolyn Marvin quotes from *The Times* in 1897 the astonishingly modern prediction, "We shall soon be nothing but transparent heaps of jelly to each other." She also quotes, from the same year, a presentation by W. E. Ayrton to the British Imperial Institute which exactly predicted the weirdness of the mobile phone, anticipating it by about a century:

> When a person wants to telegraph a friend, he knows not where, he will call in an electromagnetic voice, which will be heard loud by him who has the electromagnetic ear, but will be silent to everyone else, he will call, "Where are you?" and the reply will come loud to the man with the electromagnetic ear, "I am at the bottom of a coal mine, or crossing the Andes, or in the middle of the Pacific."

My point is, we have to place our annoyance at the mobile phone in this context. For over a hundred years, we have been pretty useless at juggling the relative claims of the *there* and the *not-there*. Perhaps that's why we are so miserable about the way people now use mobiles in public: it reminds us that we didn't deal with this problem adequately when it first arose. We let things slide. We pretended it didn't matter. We loved the phone too much to care. But phones have always obtruded; they have always trapped us in their tracker beams and transported us instantaneously to another planet. A phone conversation, being both blind and one-to-one, is a more intense and concentrated form of communication than talking face-to-face. Inevitably, then, when a phone call competes for attention with a real-world conversation, it wins. Everyone knows the distinctive high-and-dry feeling of being abandoned for a phone call, and of having to compensate – with quite elaborate behaviours – for the sudden half-disappearance of the person we were just speaking to. "Go ahead!" we say. "Don't mind us! Oh look, here's a magazine I can read!" When the call is over, other rituals come into play, to minimise the disruption caused, and to restore good feeling. "Oh, it was your *mother*, was it? Well, I wondered, naturally, but I wasn't really listening."

And now people are yelling, "So I said to her, no nails!" or "That last lot was like bog paper!" down their mobile phones in public places, and we don't know what to do about it besides boil and seethe. If only you could ignore it. In fact, why *can't* you ignore it? Do you see how the person sitting next to the caller – their boyfriend, their mum – is usually quite happily gazing out of the window or doing a word-search puzzle? Why are they so unaffected? Isn't that a bit perverse of them? What's going on?

Well, let's say you are with someone you know, at his house or in his office, and he has to take a phone call. A void opens up, doesn't it? It's a kind of limbo. A positive becomes, as it were, a temporary negative. You were plus a person; now you are minus a person. While the phone call unfolds, you sympathetically adopt a minus position yourself. When it's over, and you get the person back, you both become positive again (i.e. both are present and aware of each other).

But when the person who goes on the phone is a stranger, it's entirely different. In a train compartment where all are strenuously activating their feeble force fields, the void, the limbo, is implicitly agreed to be the desired state of all. Then the phone rings, a young woman answers it, and a bizarre thing happens: she duly absents herself from her surroundings, but the result is not a double negative, as you might suppose. She becomes a positive! "Ange! I was gonna phone ya! Wha' appened? Djoo gow off wiv im?" Yes, two negatives make an intensely annoying positive! Not only that, but her sudden vivid presence demands that everyone else become positive too, hanging on every word. It's awful. The old healing rituals don't apply in this situation, since there is no conciliatory "Do you mind?" beforehand, or explanatory "That was my mother" afterwards. And a different, unsatisfactory kind of positive is achieved, in any case. You are now intensely aware of this intensely present woman. "Yer, well, she's a slag in't she?" But of course she is not remotely aware of you.

! # ⋆ !

Why don't we object more often? Why is advice on this issue always facetious, unrealistic, and only weakly amusing?

"Switch on a tape recorder and place it in front of the person speaking. They will soon shut up."

"Note down their number and call it immediately, pretending to be someone from the office."

"When they have loudly broadcast their address and credit card details, text this information to them with the accompanying message, For God's sake, we can all hear you, shut up."

"Wait for the call to finish, then go over and start talking to the user, but *just mouth the words*."

"Pick up their phone and throw it out of the window."

There are many reasons why we don't do these things. Ingrained politeness and fear of reprisal are prominent among them. Also, any fair-minded person is bound to ask, "Why am I taking this personally? I know perfectly well that it's not personal." So we grumble and sigh and fidget, and occasionally catch the eye of another passenger similarly fed up, because we feel that a public space should be neutral and shared. We don't want to dominate it ourselves; we just don't want anyone else to dominate it, either – and the idea of people being able to tune in to telly stations on the underground drives me close to despair. In that *New York Times* story of the business-reply envelope guerrilla, there is a tantalising reference to illegal hand-held "jammers" that can block all phone signals in a forty-five-foot radius; also a gadget called "TV-B-Gone", which can switch off televisions, rather as the name implies. I am urgently in the market for both these wonderful inventions – especially if they operate secretly, as I am getting quite bold (not to say stroppy) in this regard already, and am generally asking for a punch in the face. I now automatically ask taxi drivers to switch off their annoying talk radio; at the self-storage warehouse, where a pop channel is left blaring amid the units for the supposed entertainment of the patrons, I just march in and unplug the hi-fi; at Broadcasting House, if I am waiting alone in reception, I switch off Radio 2. When I am thwarted in my mission to restore neutral quiet to public areas, by the way, I get quite confused. "Anyone listening to this?" I said the other day in the dentist's waiting-room, finger already poised above the "Off" button (which wasn't easy, as the hi-fi was fixed quite high up on the wall). "Yes, I am," said a woman. I was completely taken aback. If she hadn't looked pained and swollen, I think I would have called her a liar.

Back with the mobile phone, however, I have started to think that the rudeness is not in answering them, because answering a ringing phone is a kind of conditioned reflex that few of us can resist. I am beginning to think it is much more rude to call one. I find that people I've never spoken to before are increasingly choosing to call me on my mobile before even checking whether I am at my desk. They then leave a message involving a lot of numbers that I'm in no position to write down. Since my mobile doesn't work properly indoors (insufficient signal), it will merely indicate that I have a message. Sighing and muttering, I have no choice but to put some shoes on, leave the house, climb a hill, and pace up and down with my eyes closed and my fist to my head. Then I come back downhill, come indoors, grab a pen and paper, go up the hill again and listen again, taking notes. When I finally get back indoors again, huffing and fuming, I reach for the phone and discover that, while I've been outside doing this Grand Old Duke of York impression for the neighbours, the bastards have called me at my desk as an afterthought.

The most touching aspect of that 1897 prediction about the electromagnetic voice communicating with the electromagnetic ear is that the voice cries out, "Where are you?" and the reply comes, so splendidly, "In the Andes!" This, of course, is the key to the universal jumping-up-and-down reaction to "I'm on the train." Surely a technology so miraculous deserves to convey communication that's a bit less banal? Other people's overheard conversations fall into four categories, it seems to me, and each carries its own objection:

1   business conversations that, in an office setting, would be conducted behind closed doors;

2   intimate conversations that ought to be conducted behind closed doors;

3   humdrum domestic arrangements which would keep perfectly well for later; and

4   dross.

All these types are uncomfortable to listen to. But it's hard to see what can be done. On the one hand, it is a natural thing in humans to communicate. Putting the mobile phone in context, with the birth of each new form of communication technology (the penny post, the postcard), there has been a similar explosion of superfluous usage, just for the hell of it. On the other hand, however, the inconsiderateness is a proper cause for concern, and in particular it highlights a new development of relations in public: that group pressure no longer operates in the way that it once did. Formerly, a person might weigh it up: I want to do this anti-social thing, but there are twenty other people here, so I won't. The calculation now is different. I want to do this anti-social thing, and if anyone objects, I'll tell him to Eff Off. I can bank on him not getting support from other people, incidentally, because that's the way things are.

The Eff-Off reflex is where we will pick up the story of modern rudeness in the next chapter. But in the meantime, there was one particular point from those news stories I want to pick up. Of course, I'm hoping that other people share my reaction to those stories, which is, broadly:

1 *The schoolgirl story*
Reaction: outrage; bit of teeth-grinding; "Not in my day", etcetera

2 *Virginia banning low-slung jeans*
Reaction: knee-jerk despair at reactionary legislation, followed by honest anxiety about my politics because, actually, I'm a bit sick of seeing young people's underwear as well

3 *Television on the tube*
Reaction: gloom; Cassandra-ish tearing of hair; searching on internet for "TV-B-Gone" and other gadgets

4  *The small revenges story*
Reaction: supportive cheering; resolve to buy strips
of sheet metal and clear all other work from routine

5  *Dealing with doorstep callers by ingenious means*
Reaction: slightly louder supportive cheering; resolve
to practise "Quick! I tied him to a kitchen chair but
he's wriggling free!"

6  *People are losing the ability to concentrate*
Reaction: self-righteous nodding and arm-folding;
muttering of, "I told you so", followed by, "Hang on,
what are we talking about, I've forgotten."

"Whatever happened to consideration?" we cry.
Well, the prerequisite of consideration is the ability
to imagine being someone other than oneself, and
that's a bit of a lost cause. For me, the detail that
springs out and alarms me most from the news
stories at the start of this chapter is the word "tolerant" in the London Underground report. *"We will focus
on education instead,"* said a spokesman. *"People need to be
told to be tolerant, so we will be running ads similar to those
found on overground trains."* The spokesman is, I think,

suggesting that those who make calls or watch TV in a crowded Northern Line carriage should be *considerate* of other passengers; oddly, however, he uses the word "tolerant" instead.

Why? Well, it is possible that he just has a small vocabulary, but it's still a significant slip. From his point of view, you see, the nuisance-makers will soon be the ones operating within their rights. Therefore, if trouble is to be avoided, the nuisance-makers are the ones who must be tolerant; they must exercise saintly forbearance when they find people around them shouting, "Turn that Effing thing off! Turn that Effing thing off! It's driving me Effing mad!" Being tolerated by selfish people who don't understand that they're in public may be the final straw for some of us. We may have no alternative – and I didn't want to get quite so gloomy when I'm only half-way through the book – but we may have no alternative but to stay home and bolt the door.

# THE FOURTH GOOD REASON

# THE FOURTH GOOD REASON

---

## The Universal Eff-Off Reflex

The world has changed a lot since the Hungarian-born George Mikes published his classic work *How to be an Alien* in 1946. What he observed about the British in those early post-war days was our habit of reserve, irony, and understatement; our determination to avert unpleasantness mainly by ignoring it. J. B. Priestley famously lamented that the difficulty of writing plays about the non-confrontational English is their refusal to "make a scene". Mikes, in his chapter "How to be Rude", nailed this trait beautifully.

> If someone tells you an obviously untrue story, on the Continent you would remark, "You are a liar, Sir, and a dirty one at that." In England you just say "Oh, is that so?" Or "That's rather an unusual story, isn't it?"

Turned down for a job as a translator, for which he was completely unqualified, Mikes was told, "I am afraid your English is somewhat unorthodox." He found this hilarious. In any other European country, he says, the equivalent brush-off would have taken the form of calling to the commissionaire, "Jean, kick this gentleman down the steps!" The proper British way is, in the words of Arnold Bennett, "always to behave as if nothing has happened, no matter what has happened". We esteem it our highest national virtue that we can look back on a day of total disaster and say, "Well, I think that went pretty well, don't you?"

The question is: why do we have such a horror of directness? Why do we place value on not saying what we mean? Why do we think it's *funny*? Why do we think the word "irony" gives us magical permission to confuse less devious foreigners about whether we're serious or not? Given that it is now commonplace to be told to Eff Off by eight-year-olds, are we just finally paying the price for confusing directness with rudeness for so long? Kate Fox, by the end of *Watching the English*, is clearly exasperated by our stubborn refusal to assert ourselves, and is convinced that the recent rise of verbal aggression is not some strange, illogical departure from traditional reserve; it is just the flipside of the same behaviour.

> We are always oblique, always playing some complex, convoluted game. When we are not doing things backwards (saying the opposite of what we mean ...), we are doing them sideways (addressing our indignant mutterings about queue-jumpers to other queuers ... rather than actually tackling the offenders). Every social situation is fraught with ambiguity, knee-deep in complication, hidden meanings, veiled power struggles, passive-aggression and paranoid confusion.

She goes on:

> When we feel uncomfortable in social situations (that is, most of the time) we either become over-polite, buttoned up and awkwardly restrained, or loud, loutish, crude, violent and generally obnoxious. Both our famous "English reserve" and our infamous "English hooliganism" are symptoms of this social dis-ease, as is our obsession with privacy.

This really is an affliction. Call it the absence of frankness. Call it passive aggression. If there is a chance that we can call a spade an everyday long-handled horticultural implement for the purpose of digging, we would genuinely prefer it. As for our cowardly attitude to quite straightforward confrontation, well, here is a story illustrative of the British–US divide. I was complaining recently to a New Yorker about a British man who annoys me by joshingly referring to me as "World-Famous Author" when we are out with mutual friends. He has a generally mocking and sardonic tone, this chap; when I'm around, his technique is to invent headlines. I might say, "Mm, I don't know what to have," and he says, "Oh. World-Famous Author *can't decide what to eat*." This gives me the utter pip. It is clearly hostile, but I feel I'm not allowed to say so. And so it goes on. "Oh, World-Famous Author *gets a haircut but isn't sure she likes it*." "World-Famous Author thinks it may be time to re-read *Great Expectations*."

Now, I think I make it plain enough that this annoys me, but of course I employ the time-honoured British method of conveying my rancour: I smile along with everyone else, and say afterwards,

"Well, how lovely to see you again. We ought to make this a regular occasion! What a card you are!" My New Yorker friend listened rather impatiently to the problem, then set me straight. And I'll admit, when he did, he scared me.

"Listen," he snapped. "What's the name of this jerk?"

"Er, Mick," I said.

"OK, this is what you do. Next time you see him, you take him to one side and you say, 'Mick. Cut it out.'"

I laughed. "I can't do that," I said.

My friend did not laugh. He was serious. "Yes you can. You say, 'Mick, cut it out, you're being an Effing jerk, and it's not funny.' Trust me, he'll stop."

I looked at him in amazement. Could it really be as simple as that? Should I just tell him to stop? I could honestly have lived to the end of my life and not come up with such a brilliant and original strategy on my own.

My suspicion is that we have to accept what very, very strange and perversely indirect people we are before we can understand where the Universal Eff-Off Reflex has come from. It is so brutally defensive, so swingeingly final, that it clearly comes, itself, out of a sense of affront and outrage. People don't expect to be spoken to directly; it is interpreted as sheer hostility. I keep thinking of an incident twenty years ago when I was travelling by train to the seaside with my sister and her children. We were in the buffet compartment, consuming crisps and drinks, when a woman came in with a dog. "Oh, that's charming!" announced my sister, folding her arms and pulling a face. "What a thing to do in a place where food is served. Stop eating, children. I suppose I'll have to throw all this food away now, won't I? And just because certain people can't read signs!" Now, this scene would play out very differently today, because what happened next was that I went over and spoke to the woman. It was, for me, an unusually assertive thing to do, but I felt it was necessary to act, if only to prevent more of this pointed harrumphing. "Excuse me," I said, "there's a notice above the door that says you can't bring dogs in here." The woman – who would nowadays, of course, tell me to Eff Off – said she was sorry and took the dog away. What has always intrigued me about this incident, however, was that my sister was horrified by what I had done. "That was so rude," she said. "Going over and speaking to that woman was so rude."

! # * !

The Universal Eff-Off Reflex is generally agreed to be something new in the world of manners. I wrote a piece in the *Daily Telegraph* while preparing this book, and I received a number of letters and emails afterwards about rudeness, a high proportion of which dealt with the holy shock of being told to Eff Off by someone they'd never met. Some people say Eff Off all the time, of course – and this is shocking and worrying enough in itself, but what I'm really interested in here is the way we are getting less and less prepared to accept criticism or admonishment, or ever to say sorry. An overtaking car endangers your life. You flash your lights. The driver makes the wanker signal at you. A pedestrian steps out in front of a bus. The bus brakes abruptly, spilling its passengers on the floor, and toots its horn. The pedestrian turns his back, holds up a finger, and saunters away. No one is ever in the wrong, it seems. If you point out to someone that he is in the wrong, you

TALK TO THE HAND

must be prepared for the consequences, which may
include violence, but will automatically include Eff
Off.

This is not just at street level, either. We are all
Teflon people, on whom criticism cannot stick.
Abuse is becoming accepted as the quickest and
smartest way of dealing with criticism in all areas
of life. I had an interesting experience in 2004 when
my book *Eats, Shoots & Leaves* received a mauling in
the *New Yorker*, and my London publisher riposted
on my behalf that the author of the critical article
was "a tosser". Now, I loved my publisher for doing
this, of course. He was defending my honour. He is
a famously maverick character. And although I have
never read the article, I have heard enough about it
to suspect that the chosen epithet actually had some
merit in this case. But good grief, how embarrassing. Meanwhile, ripostes of this sort made by public
figures are reported in the news, and quoted as if
they were witty or thoughtful. In April 2005, when
the football manager Harry Redknapp was heckled
and booed at Portsmouth, he was reported as saying,
"If people have got nothing better to do than shout
abuse at me, they must have sad lives, and I feel sorry

for them." And I repeat, *this was on the news*.

So there are several things contributing to the Universal Eff-Off Reflex. The state of manners is driving some of us to be direct, which makes us uncomfortable enough in the first place. And this directness is whacked straight back at us by people who are never in the wrong, who interpret direct-ness as sheer hostility, and who say Eff Off so much in their normal conversations anyway that it springs automatically to their cherry-red lips. The prison psychiatrist Theodore Dalrymple (whom we shall meet again in chapter six) notes, in his book *Life at the Bottom* (2001), that Eff Off is a favourite tattoo among the people he meets.

> Why anyone should want these words indelibly imprinted on his skin is a mystery whose meaning I have not yet penetrated ... but I recall a patient who had the two words tattooed in mirror writing upon his forehead, no doubt that he might read them in the bathroom mirror every morning and be reminded of the vanity of earthly concerns.

But why don't people take the criticism on board? Why doesn't telling-off *work*? I'm sure it used to. In the past, if someone was so offended by your actions that they broke the directness taboo, you would take it to heart. You felt *ashamed*.

Now, you may remember that Norbert Elias identified shame as one of the twin engines of the civilising process. Shame is now such a quaint, bygone concept that one feels almost embarrassed to bring it up. "Have you no *shame*?" is a question merrily kicked aside; indeed, shamelessness is not only a highly regarded modern attribute, but the *sine qua non* of most successful TV and entertainment formats, which compete to push shamelessness to ever further limits. Things used to be different. My own childhood, and the childhood of many others of my generation, was marked by episodes of this red-hot, moiling state of self-blame, and I am not going to say it never did me any harm. I am obliged to admit, on the contrary, that it left me so psychologically flailed, scorched, eviscerated, and hobbled that it's a miracle I can drag myself about.

I can appreciate, therefore, why modern parents would want to shield their own children from such a terrible awareness of personal worthlessness. But surely they go too far? Modern parents from all classes seem genuinely to believe they are doing the right thing by protecting their children from blame or accountability of any sort. Every time the little chaps get themselves on a hook, the parents gently lift them down and tell them to run along and forget about it. While working-class parents pride themselves on how quickly they can march to the school and pin a teacher against a blackboard, middle-class people spend a lot of time worrying, "Is it right to tell off other people's children?" and wringing their hands amid the shards of their favourite Chinese jardinière. This is one of the big etiquette dilemmas of our times. Families arrive at your house and you wait for the parents to say, "Remember, children, this is Uncle Robert's house, and it has lovely things in it that don't belong to you. So please be very good and don't touch anything." But they don't do this. They say, "Say hi to Bob, kids. Yes, darling, this is the man we call Fatty Bob, how clever you are to remember. Now, why don't you all run off and see how many things beginning with the letter H you can collect for mummy? All right, Freddie, you can use a screwdriver. Take your sticky drinks with you, darlings, that's right." Later, if you confront a child with its bad behaviour, the parents will step in at once. "Fatty Bob didn't mean to be nasty to you, darling. He's just a bit materialistic, which means he prefers things to people. *We* prefer people to things, don't we? Besides, Fatty Bob shouldn't leave such irreplaceable heirlooms just lying about, should he? Silly Fatty Bob."

So what is shame? Why is it socially useful? Elias defines shame as an "anxiety" and explains it as a sophisticated act of self-division, when a person is forced to judge his own behaviour against an internal moral censor ("the sector of his consciousness by which he controls himself"). The idea is that we import a sense of social opinion, internalise it, and measure ourselves against it. But he isn't talking about judging oneself on a scale of good–bad. Interestingly, what Elias sees in shame is that we place ourselves on a scale of superior–inferior, which is probably much, much harder to take. "It is a conflict within his own personality; he himself recognizes himself as inferior ... This is what makes him so defenceless against gestures of superiority by others which somehow trigger off this automatism within him."

Saying sorry involves the same sort of process.

Taking Erving Goffman's "splitting" description of apology, it seems that this division now takes place a lot less than it used to. People have been brought up not to split under any circumstances – least of all when an apology is demanded. Quite the reverse. Under attack, the individual personality wastes no time bolstering its defences. It circles the wagons and starts firing. Not a second is allowed for self-examination. Where this comes out in a most peculiar way is in our dealings with people who, we feel, are obliged to apologise on behalf of the company they represent, but who don't see how they are personally involved. My favourite story from the many sent in by *Daily Telegraph* readers concerned a man buying a book. He had entered a reputable bookshop and been treated in an off-hand manner when he asked for help. Then, having located the book, he paid for it with his credit card. The assistant put the bill in the bag, and he said, "I'd like to put the bill separately, please," at which he was told, "Well, you know where it is; you can do that yourself." He felt aggrieved, and said so. "I've been in this shop for five minutes and spent thirty pounds, and no one has been polite to me." At which the assistant retaliated,

"Just because you spent thirty pounds doesn't mean you've *bought my soul.*"

! # ⋆ !

Deference is a topic for another chapter. What I think marks out the Universal Eff-Off Reflex is contained in the name: it's a reflex. It's as if you touch someone lightly on the shoulder and *snick, snack,* the next thing you know, your hand has been severed at the wrist. It is startling partly because it's so primitive, so *animal.* Through shielding children from feelings of low self-worth, we have created people who simply will not stand to be corrected in any way. "Excuse me, I think you dropped this," you say. "Eff Off," they say, with heat. "There ought to be an apostrophe on that sign." "Eff Off." A contestant on a quiz who is told, "The answer to 'Who wrote *Pride and Prejudice?*' was Jane Austen" will not bite a lip and look embarrassed. He will say, "I didn't know that because it's not a thing worth knowing!" – and get a little cheer from the audience for sticking up for himself.

But the last aspect of the Universal Eff-Off Reflex I want to consider is just why so many of us are speaking up anyway. "Don't cycle on the pavement, you hooligan!" we shout, even though experience now tells us that it's dangerous, and our built-in inhibition begs us not to. Moreover, we are beginning to realise that if we appeal for other people to agree with us, they will either make themselves scarce or concentrate very hard on a bit of urgent texting. Whatever happened to our famous controlling characteristic of "negative politeness" – of minding one's own business?

Back with George Mikes, he wrote several follow-up books to *How to be an Alien*, including *How to be Inimitable* (1960). All the books are collected in *How to be a Brit*. This is how he describes British non-confrontational habits forty-five years ago, in his chapter, "On Minding One's Own Business":

> If a man happens to be standing on your foot in the bus, you must not ask him to get off, since it is clearly his business where he chooses to stand; if your neighbour's television or radio is blaring military marches till midnight, you may not remonstrate with him because it is his business what he pleases to listen to and at what time; if you are walking peacefully in the street and

someone pours two gallons of boiling water over
your best bowler through his bathroom overflow
... you should proceed without uttering a word
– however short – because it is obviously the other
fellow's business when he has his bath and how
hot he likes it.

I have an awful feeling that I used to agree with
this. Now, however, it is unrecognisable as British
behaviour. Personally, I have turned into a bug-eyed
mad person who must either speak up or explode
– which is as much of a departure from previous
norms as the Eff-Off Reflex is. For example, I was
recently in a check-out queue, being served by a
young woman. From his place at the next till, an
odious boy of about seventeen was loudly and unself-
consciously telling her the story of a friend who had
discovered the decomposing body of an old woman
in her house. "She hadn't been seen for *seven days*,"
he said, at the beginning, with all the relish of the fat
boy in Dickens who wants to make your flesh creep.
As he absently scanned somebody else's shopping
– Whiskas, Double Gloucester, etcetera – it became
obvious that no detail was going to be omitted from
his grisly tale.

I didn't know what to do. This situation offended me on so many levels. For a start, the two of them were ignoring their customers. Yet the woman who was being served by the boy (and who had far more right than me to be offended) seemed unconcerned. If anything, she was amused. The girl at my till just rolled her eyes at me, as if to say, "What can you do?" Again, I don't think she was remotely bothered by the content of the story, or struck by its inappropriateness; she merely thought the boy was a bit of a tosser. So he had just described the bluebottles buzzing in the curtained window, and the door being broken down, and the smell coming out, when I finally broke. "Stop telling that story, for pity's sake!" I said. The boy stopped. His customer pulled a face and shrugged. Looking back, I suppose I'm lucky that nobody actually laughed. As far as I was concerned, I could not possibly mind my own business in this situation. I had to say something. But having done so, I have never felt so alone and alienated in my life.

Drugs are probably the only solution, unfortunately. Strong, mood-altering drugs will ultimately stop me from Speaking Up. It was the same with being a stickler for punctuation, of course. It's the same urge to correct the world, and drag it into line; and it is bound to be met with the same consternation. Look into the eyes of someone who is telling you to Eff Off and what you will often find there, along with aggression, is pure surprise. "What's up with *her*?" the look says. "Where did *that* spring from?" For the boy at the check-out, when I yelled at him, it was as if a tin of beans had suddenly jumped up from the conveyor belt and biffed him in the eye; unaware of anyone else within ear-shot, he believed he was having a private conversation. Why couldn't I mind my own business? Why had I broken the basic rules of "negative politeness"? Why had I been so *rude*?

There is one positive aspect to all this. It's quite a feeble one, but worth mentioning. Even though there were hundreds of complaints from BBC viewers about the swearing at the Live8 concert, the word Eff every day loses some of its shock power. I would still be horrified to hear my mum say it, and I always apologise to her if I let it slip out when I'm talking to her, but it's clearly the case that through sheer constant over-use, "Effing" is becoming a meaningless intensifier and will soon hardly be worth saying. There is a hilarious section about gossip in *Watching the English*, in which the three ways an English man can react to news are anatomised:

1 with surprise
2 with anger
3 with elation and triumph

In each case, Kate Fox explains, "expletives" must be used. In other words, he can say:

1 "Effing hell!"
2 "Oh, Eff that!"
3 "Eff, yes! Effing fantastic!"

And they say the language of Shakespeare and Milton is dead. Television, as always, delights in accelerating the process of social change by normalising the entertainingly shocking. In the first five minutes of a recent *Gordon Ramsay's Kitchen Nightmares*, the famously robust chef said:

> You are Effing useless, this is Effing disgusting, this is Effing frozen in the centre, it's as authentic

as an Effing Chinese takeaway, that was Effing dire,
you're giving the customer Effing food poisoning,
I am so Effing glad the customers can't see what's
going on, I don't know where to Effing start.

Well, strike that man's head a glancing blow
with a frying pan, but I suppose he is ultimately
serving the greater good, even if he doesn't know
it. *Blue Peter* viewers wait for the day a children's TV
presenter says with a big smile, "And now it's time
to make an Effing model car park out of an Effing
corn-flake packet!" At that point, all-clear sirens will
sound throughout the land and the reign of Eff will
be officially over. By great good fortune, the word
that is far more shocking than Eff – you probably
know the one I mean – can't really step up to take its
place, being an incontrovertible noun with far less
scope for use as a verb, adverb, adjective and intensifier. Tee hee. Those Effing Eff people may know Eff
All about grammar, but grammar will ultimately Eff
them in the end.

Wasn't it amusing, incidentally, that when Jerry
Springer briefly visited the UK to make a British
version of his show, he was reportedly astonished
by the amount of foul language he heard? Perhaps,

in common with many other Americans, he thought that in Britain we talked like something out of *Mary Poppins*. He thought we said things like, "Stripe me pink, I am proper peeved and no mistake. Do you know, I'd like to give that scallywag a piece of my mind. Heavens, yes indeedy." In fact, of course, it's easier to shield yourself from bad language in America than it is here. There is an old joke about an English tourist asking a New York taxi-driver, "Excuse me, can you tell me the way to Carnegie Hall, or shall I just go and Eff myself?" Nowadays the joke works better with an American asking the way to Piccadilly Circus.

In the meantime, however, the Universal Eff-Off Reflex looks set to stay and I am clearly destined to keep running foul of it. Each of us is inside a bubble, after all. Most of us grow more grumpy and misanthropic every day. Pascal said, "I have discovered that all human misery comes from a single thing, which is not knowing enough to stay quietly in your room." Sometimes I have a little dream that it is eight o'clock on a fine wintry morning, and as I leave my house to walk to the station, I notice I'm feeling rather light-hearted. No one about. No cars. No noise except the faraway hum of a milk float. Mm. Nice. The street is clean as if washed by recent rain. I walk briskly, humming to myself, cross a quiet road and arrive at the station in good time for the 8.49. As I buy my paper (putting coins in a slot), I notice that the concourse is empty, utterly empty, and I begin to think well, this is a bit too good to be true, but never mind, they cleared Times Square for Tom Cruise that time, didn't they? And *Vanilla Sky* was rubbish. I buy a ticket (no queue), board the train (no other passengers), and feel blissfully happy.

Now, this may be a dream, I think, as the train begins to move. This may even be – and that distant milk float was rather a giveaway – a long-forgotten episode of *The Avengers* that has somehow lodged in my brain and is now repeating itself as a kind of benign near-death experience as I lie unconscious at the bottom of some stairs. Either way, I don't care. Somehow, overnight, other people have been eradicated, expunged, annihilated, or just ordered to stay indoors and keep out of my bloody way. And you know how it feels? It feels *right*.

# THE FIFTH GOOD REASON

# THE FIFTH GOOD REASON

## Booing the Judges

A young woman of my acquaintance once wrote to Tommy Steele. You may remember him from such films as *Half a Sixpence* and such chart-topping songs as "Little White Bull". For many years, he lived in a rather grand eighteenth-century house behind a high wall on the main road between Richmond and Kingston in Surrey, near to where I grew up, and we council-estate locals were jolly pleased to have him in the neighbourhood, even though we never actually saw him. Whenever the song "'Old it flash bang wallop what a picture!" was played on *Two-Way Family Favourites*, we turned up the volume with a glow of pride. Anyway, one day, about fifteen years ago, this young woman wrote to him, but it was not a fan letter. It was an accusation, expressed in quite belligerent terms. "I have been past your house on the top deck of a bus for years and years," she wrote, "yet I have never seen you. As a famous person, don't you have a duty to appear for people? You'd be nobody without us, you know." Unbelievably, she received a reply. Tommy Steele wrote to say that, if she cared to catch a bus on Sunday afternoon between two and three, he would be in the garden and would give her a wave. "Well, was he there?" I asked, when she told me about it, some months later. She snorted with laughter. "How should I know?" she said. "I didn't *go*."

When people applaud the "end of deference" in our society, they tend to evoke the old British class system, with its sepia-coloured peasants clutching cloth caps to their waistcoats and refusing to make a fuss about dying of industrial chest ailments. Words such as "servile" and "repressive" crop up, as the bad old days are given a glad good riddance. People will even resort (as I did, earlier) to the slightly dubious argument that posh people are quite unworthy of special respect, in any case, being genetically stupid from the in-breeding, laughably out of touch with popular entertainment, apt to pelt each other with bakery products in London's club land, and absolute bastards where foxes are concerned. The end of deference is presented as politically progressive and therefore a good thing. Nobody "looks up" to anyone any more: Hooray! The media don't allow anyone to get too big for their boots: Hooray! In the bad old days ordinary people often had to cope with feelings of inferiority, which sometimes drove them to exert themselves: Boo! But now we have relativism and entitlement: Hooray! Oh yes, everything is grandy and dandy. Hooray, hooray, hooray!

What a brave new world we have, then, that glorifies rudeness in the name of egalitarianism. The British have always enjoyed the sport of abusing public figures; we regard it as hilarious as well as cathartic. I was once at Madison Square Garden in New York, to report on a heavyweight title bout between Lennox Lewis and Evander Holyfield, and yes, I know how odd that sounds, but this isn't the place to explain. The point is that, before the fight, the ring announcer made a fatal error: addressing a crowd with a large, rowdy British element, he listed the celebrities in the audience. He evidently thought we would be impressed. "Ladies and gentlemen, we have Paul Simon in the Garden tonight!" he said.

And what happened? "Booo!" yelled the Brits. "We have John Kennedy Junior!" "BOOOO!" "We have Michael Douglas!" "BOOOO!" Only two people were given a cheer by the British contingent: Jack Nicholson and Keith Richards. I felt embarrassed by my chippy countrymen. Abuse is the weapon of the weak. But at the same time, I did feel very proud. I mean, I like Paul Simon. I have nothing against him. But nobody deserves uncritical acclaim just for filling a ringside seat at a punch-up.

This traditional weapon of the weak is, however, becoming heavier and more blunt. There seems to be an avid and self-righteous movement to make public figures pay the price for too much deference in the past. It is getting a bit bloody. The royal family is brutally cut down to size whenever the opportunity arises, and you certainly don't have to be Jeremy Paxman any more to be rude to a politician. In fact, if you see John Prescott in a motorway service station, the accepted MO seems to be that first you insult him, then you go and get a bunch of friends in hoods with a video camera so that you can perform a "happy slap" (i.e., a filmed assault). As for famous people – well, who the hell would want to be famous any more? You'd have to be insane. People demand you appear for them in your garden, and then they don't even show up to give you a wave. On a recent *Have I Got News for You*, Les Dennis told the story of a celebrity (whose name meant nothing to me) being struck in the street by a woman with an umbrella, who then said, "You see? I told you it was him!" There is a well-worn dictum that, in Britain, "they build you up and then they tear you down", but it's getting to the point where the tearing-down is far too much fun to hang about for. There was once a story in *Private Eye* about a bloodsports enthusiast so excited by the delivery of some pheasant chicks that he shot them in the box. This is, I think, a pretty good image for the way public life now works in this country.

All this would be all right if it actually served the cause of egalitarianism, but it plainly doesn't. Look around. We don't even have social mobility any more. Just because newspapers refer to HRH The Prince of Wales as "Chazza" (and everyone feels free to say vile things about his uncomplaining wife) does not make him the same as you and me. There seems to be an idea that the more disrespect you show towards the rich or famous (for example, squirting water in the face of Tom Cruise), the nearer you move towards achieving equality, but the effect is quite the opposite: rudeness highlights difference. In a truly egalitarian society, everyone would show respect to everyone else. It is very bad news for our society that overt disrespect is such a big game these days, because it just stirs people up without enlightening them. Mass entertainment that demeans public figures satisfies popular base instincts but leaves nobody better off. Besides, at the same time as it's become fashionable never to look up to anyone, it has become nastily acceptable to *look down*.

The "end of deference" is about a lot more than the flattening of class distinctions, in any case. This is where the baby has been so thoughtlessly poured down the drain with the bath water. Respect and consideration are traditionally due to other people for all sorts of reasons, some big, some small. Here are twenty (mostly lapsed) reasons to show special politeness to other people that have nothing to do with class.

1 they are older
2 they know more than you do

3   they know less than you do
4   they got here first
5   they have educational qualifications in the subject under discussion
6   you are in their house
7   they once helped you financially
8   they have been good to you all your life
9   they are less fortunate than you
10  they have achieved status in the wider world
11  you are serving them in a shop
12  they are in the right
13  they are your boss
14  they work for you
15  they are a policeman/teacher/doctor/judge
16  they are in need
17  they are doing you a favour
18  they paid for the tickets
19  you phoned them, not the other way round
20  they have a menial job

The utter bloody rudeness of the world today is about a lot of things, as we have already seen, but I think what most dismays many honourable people is the way "deference" has become a dirty little demeaning word, while its close relative "respect" has become a cool street-crime buzz-word mainly associated with paying feudal obeisance to those in possession of firearms. Both words have lost their true meaning. Deference is not about lying down and letting someone put their foot on your head. It is not about kow-tow. It is about assessing what is due to other people on all sorts of grounds. The dictionary definition of "in deference to" is: "out of respect for; in consideration of". To show deference does not mean "I hereby declare I am inferior to you." But that's what people seem to think it means, so they refuse to defer to anybody, on any grounds at all. The same misunderstanding prevents people from apologising. They think that if they say "Sorry", it means "I am 100 per cent to blame. And now that I've admitted it, you can sue the pants off me."

! # * !

Contempt is the word. Although I don't know why I bother continuing with this; most of you are too stupid to follow it, let's be honest. All right, I suppose I'll have to spell it out. Contempt, also known as "attitude", is the new behavioural default mode. And what breeds contempt? Oh, come on, you muppets! I'm working with idiots here. What breeds contempt? Familiarity! Blimey, I thought you were cleverer than that, mate. Although judging by the way you've been moving your lips while you read this, I don't know where I got *that* idea.

It goes against the grain just to sit here applauding the sagacity of a proverb, but I find that I have no choice. So here goes. What breeds contempt? Familiarity breeds contempt. I used to be confused by this saying, incidentally, because I thought it meant "familiarity" in the sense of being familiar with the lay-out of Exeter, or familiar with the problem plays of Shakespeare, and I thought, "Hang on, the more I know about *Measure for Measure*, the more I admire it! When Claudio pleads so eloquently for his life at the expense of his sister's chastity, I am absolutely fit to be tied. And that Cathedral Close in Exeter is lovely. Familiarity really boosts things in one's estimation. What on earth are these proverb-coiners talking about?"

But it isn't that kind of familiarity. It's the sort that has you call your maths teacher "Jeff". It's going up to the Prime Minister and saying, "Nice jacket; how much?" It is using someone's loo without asking, and leaving the seat up as evidence. It is calling someone you've never met, on their mobile, to settle a dispute about punctuation. Few issues divide generations more than the issue of familiarity. It is one of the main rudenesses cited by older people, and it is easy to see why. People who have spent their whole lives as "Mr Webster" or "Mrs Owen" do not want to find, at the ends of their lives, that younger people who don't know them are calling them "Alf" and "Joyce". To them, it is sheer impertinence (and usually takes place when they are in a weakened state, which makes it all the more insensitive). Sometimes you really do have to admire the French. They would never stand for this kind of thing. An American writer-friend who is quite proficient in French once attempted to use a slang term with a record-shop owner, and the chap did not let it pass. "Have we *met*?" he asked, horrified at the breach of decorum.

Several of my *Daily Telegraph* correspondents objected to being called "mate" or "love" by strangers, and one particularly loathed being served in restaurants with the words "There you go." Which for some reason, always makes me laugh, because I can picture the scene: man waiting for roast dinner to be served, pouring wine for wife, practising deep breathing. "He might not say it, dear," whispers the wife, patting his hand. "I know. Don't go on about it," says the man, biting his lip. Along come two plates of dinner. "There you go!" says the waiter. "Aaaagh!" yells the man. I would include "No problem" alongside "There you go" under the heading "Unacceptable Insouciance", incidentally. I always want to administer a clip round the ear to people who accept my thanks with "No problem". The "There you go" man and I ought to go out together, I realise. We could spend most of our time jumping up and down, ranting. "*Where* do I go? Just tell me, *where do I go*? Did I *ask* whether it was a problem? Was a problem *ever mentioned*?"

It is tempting to blame the parents and the teachers for this end-of-deference state of affairs, and do you know what? I am not going to resist that temptation. As a non-parent, I naturally feel I am writing with one hand tied behind my back: after all, many of my best friends are parents, and I know they have done their best. But if I had both hands tied behind my back, I would be obliged to type this with my nose: those damned breeders know they should carry the can, so why pretend otherwise? They have let their kids manipulate, insult and bully them. They have taught them to demand respect, but not to show it. And by doing this, they have failed the kids as much as they have failed the rest of us. There is a great exchange in Arthur Miller's *Death of a Salesman* when Willy says proudly of his sons, "Two fearless characters!" and Charley dryly remarks, "The jails are full of fearless characters." Many parents nowadays seem to share Willy's view – that if a child has reached maturity and is not intimidated by anyone or anything, a fine job of parenting has been done. Who cares if the result is a generation of unhappy sociopaths? Just so long as the unhappy sociopaths regard their parents as their pals.

However, there is a big plus side to the breakdown of formality. Every day I have an encounter of some kind that is friendlier than it would have been ten years ago. The painter who decorated my living room chatted to me about his cats, which was nice. At the station, the person selling tickets says, "That's a nice bag." Not standing on ceremony softens the edges of a sharp world, perhaps? As someone who sits at home all day, banging a keyboard, I am quite grateful for a bit of friendly contact on the phone, even if the chumminess is ultimately empty of meaning, and even if I leap on it with disproportionate gratitude. For example, I give my address to a ticket agency man and he says, "Hey, I know that street. I used to live just round the corner in Buckingham Place!" and I say, "Were you at University down here?" and he says, "No, actually, I worked at the dog track" and I say, "That's really interesting" and he says, "That'll be £88 including the booking fee" and I say, "What's it like at the dog track? I've never been," and he says, "These tickets are non-refundable, and your booking reference is 127565," and I say, "Great. Well, nice to talk to you. And if you ever find yourself in Buckingham Place on a visit to old friends, or just to see the sea, ha ha, there'll be a cup of tea waiting for you at my house, absolutely, just quote booking reference 127565, hello, hello, oh he's gone, oh well." And I'm not making it up; that's the sort of fleeting human contact that can really make my day.

However, it does sometimes go wrong. I recently had a rather instructive friendly cold call from my gas supplier – instructive because it turned out to be extremely complicated, from the familiarity point of view. First of all, you see, the chap was very polite. He apologised for calling me at home, and addressed me as "Miss Truss" throughout. This kept me in a state of placation, obviously. He explained that he was calling about domestic appliance insurance, and asked if this was a good time to talk. Here are the bare bones of what happened next. I said no, sorry, writing book, can't talk. If you must ring back, give it month.

HIM: OK, fair enough.

ME: Bye.

HIM: Writing book, you say?

ME: Yes.

HIM: Mm. Well, Miss Truss, that's v. interesting. I'm bit of writer myself.

ME: Really? (*Thinks*) Oh no.

HIM: Written rather good story, wondering how to proceed. Any ideas?

ME (*incredulous, thinks*): Didn't I just say v. busy?

ME: Er, quite busy.

HIM: Appreciate anything. V. tough starting out.

ME (*deep breath; save document; turn attention*): OK, buster, here's deal. Get latest *Writer's Handbook*. Blah blah. Maybe join writing group. Send to agent. Blah blah. Copyright first? Ha ha, are you kidding, you must be kidding. Right. Not kidding. OK, send part of it, précis rest. Blah blah. Send to magazine. How long story? Well, too long BBC. Two thousand two hundred tops. Shorten it poss? Course not. Not poss. That's it. Sorry. Blah blah. Good luck. Blah blah. Hope it helps. Bye.

HIM: That's very helpful, Miss Truss. Thank you. What's your book then?

ME (*big sigh; growing impatient*): About rudeness. Big rant. Short. No discernible value. Oh, look at time. Must rush. Still on chap five.

HIM: That sounds very interesting, Miss Truss. Now, would it be rude if I point out that for as little as 38 pence a week, *which is less than the price of a Yorkie bar*, you could insure all your domestic appliances with us this afternoon?

! # * !

A bulldozer has knocked down a myriad fine
distinctions that used to pertain. I deliberately
omitted gender from my list of twenty ("they are a
member of the weaker sex"), but it's clear that many
men are particularly upset that when they show traditional politeness to women nowadays, it's a form
of Gallantry Russian Roulette. One time in six, their
courtesy makes someone's day. Four times out of six,
they get a lecture in gender politics. And one in six,
they get their heads blown off. "Are you holding that
door open because I'm a woman?" they are asked,
aggressively. And the clever ones respond, "No, I'm
doing it because I am a gentleman." The problem is,
many of the old forms of politeness (such as addressing slaves by their first names) are better abandoned,
because they were designed to serve inequality. I
was outraged recently when a bill was divided after
a rather jolly group dinner, and I was told, "Only
the men need pay." While I'm sure there were good
intentions behind this, I was furious and made quite
a noise, which was awkward for everybody – especially, I have to say, for the more easy-going women

who had already said, "Great! Thanks!" and put their bags back on the floor.

In some ways it's quite proper that we should all walk permanently on egg-shells. But it is still tiresomely hard to do the right thing. Give up your seat to a pregnant woman and she will thank you. Give up your seat to a woman who just *looks* pregnant, and she may punch you on the nose. I have started agonising on the train because I happen to know that people sitting in first-class compartments without first-class tickets run the risk of being fined on the spot. There are ugly scenes when this happens. The fine is large, and there ought to be a warning notice, but there isn't. I am thinking of writing to a problem page. How can I inform my fellow passengers of this without giving offence? My inference would be too obvious. "Excuse me, you look like a hard-up person/scoundrel/fare dodger/idiot. Allow me to give you a tip."

Thus our good intentions are often thwarted by fear in today's politically sensitive world. Offence is so easily given. And where the "minority" issue is involved, the rules seem to shift about: most of the time, a person who is female/black/disabled/

gay wants this *not* to be their defining characteris-tic; you are supposed to be blind to it. But then, on other occasions, you are supposed to observe special sensitivity, or show special respect. I was recently given a lift by a friend who thoughtfully reversed at a road junction to allow a motorised wheelchair to cross. But having done this highly decent thing, for which he was smilingly thanked, he worried about it. "I shouldn't have done that," he said. "Why, was there someone behind you?" I asked, confused. "No," he said, "but I wouldn't have done that for someone who *wasn't* disabled, would I?"

I mention all this because "political correctness" is sometimes confused with respect, but it operates quite differently. It is not about paying due regard to other people for their individual qualities, needs, or virtues; it's mainly about covering oneself and avoid-ing prosecution in a world of hair-trigger sensitivity. Hence the escalation of euphemism, and the moral panic that breaks out when a public figure uses the word "niggardly" in a perfectly correct way. In a hundred years' time, anyone wanting to know the moral contortions necessary to well-intentioned and intelligent people in the first years of the twenty-first century should just buy a DVD set of Larry David's *Curb Your Enthusiasm* – and I hope they will laugh, but there's no guarantee that things won't be a whole lot worse by then. Robert Hughes, in his 1993 book *Culture of Complaint: The Fraying of America*, writes, "It's as though all human encounter were one big sore spot, inflamed with opportunities to unwittingly give, and truculently receive, offence ... We want to create a sort of linguistic Lourdes, where evil and misfortune are dispelled by a dip in the waters of euphemism." And I would say, "Amen" to that, if it didn't potentially offend people of other faiths who employ a different form of holy affirmation.

What is left of pure deference? In Britain, I think the last thing we do well (and beautifully) is pay respects to the war dead. "When this goes, it all goes," I have started to think. The controlled emotion of Armistice Day tugs at conscience, swells the commonality of sorrow, and swivels the historical telescope to a proper angle, so that we see, however briefly, that we are not self-made: we owe an absolute debt to other people; a debt that our most solemn respect may acknowledge but can never repay. We stop and we silently remember.

Personally, I sob. I am sobbing now. It is a miracle that some sort of political relativism has not contaminated this ceremony of public grief, a full sixty years after the end of the Second World War. The first cannon fires at 11am, and one is overwhelmed by a sense of sheer humility, sheer *perspective*. We are particles of suffering humanity. For two minutes a year, it's not a bad thing to remember that. If we looked inside ourselves and remembered how insignificant we are, just for a couple of minutes a day, respect for other people would be an automatic result.

! # * !

Of the many reasons for retaining a little bit of deference and respect, the most compelling, I think, must be this common-sense appeal to self-interest. It is a well-observed fact that people are happier when they have some idea of where they stand and what the rules are. It's a basic-instinct, primal-chimp thing that is the basis of many vivid behavioural experiments. Tell an orang-utan that he answers to no one and in a couple of weeks he's lost all idea of himself. His eyes roll back, he bangs his head against trees, he eats his own deposits and wears his hair just any old how. Similarly, when people have no "boundaries" or discipline, they can't relax and it drives them nuts. Every so often, a television experiment will place ungovernable modern schoolchildren in a mocked up old-fashioned school with bells and a merit system, and they not only visibly flourish and calm down, they even learn the capital of Iceland and a bit of Latin grammar. Virtually every day on television, unruly toddlers undergo miraculous transformations when their parents are taught to stop ingratiating themselves and start imposing discipline. Not having respect for other people is clearly incredibly tiring and alienating, if only because the ego never gets a rest.

Of course, with "knowing one's place", we are flirting with class issues again. One of the traditional functions of manners was, obviously, to identify an individual with his own social group. The way you crooked your little finger when raising a tea-cup betokened either your solidarity with other people who crooked their little finger in precisely the same way, or your superiority over those who tipped the tea in the saucer and slurped happily from that. According to the famous "U" and "Non-U" system (coined by Professor Alan Ross to identify upper-class usage and popularised by Nancy Mitford), people who said "lavatory" were better than those who said "toilet". People who had fish-knives were beneath contempt. It was ever so common to say "ever so". This has largely passed, of course. In a very short time, snobbery based on vocabulary and the milk-first/milk-second issue has virtually disappeared. Honestly, you can say "serviette" at me all day until you are blue in the face, and I promise I won't even flinch.

But something useful got lost with all this. Surely one of the reasons that rudeness is such a huge issue for people today is that we worry about it more; it is a source of anxiety. We recount situations to each other, just to check our own reactions. "Was that rude? I thought that was rude. Do *you* think that's rude? Oh thank goodness you agree with me, because I thought it was rude but then I thought maybe I was being over-sensitive." I mentioned Larry David's *Curb Your Enthusiasm* earlier, because every episode entails anxiety over what's acceptable in a world where people are free to disagree, but still hold fiercely to their own rules. There is a whole episode, for example, about "cut-off time". Someone tells Larry you can't call people at home after 10pm. Is that true? It can't be true. How can that be a *rule*? He tries it and gets into trouble. The next night he calls someone before 10pm and gets into trouble because *their* cut-off time is 9.30. Rules exist, it seems, but there are no rules about the rules. This, in a nutshell, is the insanity of the modern condition.

But how can we go back? As Mark Caldwell points out, in his *Short History of Rudeness*, many rules of etiquette are mere conventions with no moral content or usefulness – which is the sort of thing we don't put up with these days. The reason table manners always played such a large part in etiquette guides was that so many of the intricate rules of eating had no other function than to trip the ignorant. Piling peas on the back of the fork is the usual example given of an etiquette rule that was contrived from the start as pure class-indicator, being otherwise daft, strange, counter-intuitive, and instrumental in letting your dinner get cold. Knives and forks were for a long time the main concern of manners guides, not to mention of posh people. There is an excellent clerihew on this subject about the Duke of Fife:

It looked bad when the Duke of Fife
Left off using a knife;
But people began to talk
When he left off using a fork.

Caldwell cites a rather extreme example of sheer class-solidarity etiquette from a sixteenth-century German chronicle: an old aristocratic Christmas tradition in which dinner companions "festively pelted each other with dog turds". No doubt this tradition arose out of one of those tragic mistranslations from scripture one is always hearing about (scholars will one day discover that the Aramaic for "dog turd" is very close to the word for "season's greetings"), but the point remains: if everyone's doing it, do it. You will be accepted by your peers. You can relax.

The tragedy is that we have swept away class snobbery largely without grasping the opportunity to respect different things. So now, in place of a hierarchy of class, or a system of respect for other people, we mainly have stuff. The glory of stuff has swept most other considerations aside. I would say that respect is now allowable in very few fields: we respect sportsmen (but only when they are playing sport), and we respect charisma, but mainly we respect anyone who's got the latest iPod. Manners guides have actually reflected this shift. Look at modern ones and you will find that instead of teaching you to consider the feelings of others, they tell you what gift to take to a dinner party, how much to spend on flowers for a wedding, and what range of social stationery to buy. In other words, how you act is less important, in terms of status, than what you have. But is this ultimately satisfying? There is a *New Yorker* cartoon that says it all. Dog says to dog: "I've got the bowl, the bone, the big yard. I know I *should* be happy."

It's not just children or members of shaven-headed bling-bling street gangs who are infected with this stuff-anxiety, either. I have sophisticated, left-leaning friends who visibly cheer up when the subject turns to designer clothes, and I have long been aware that my refusal to care about clothes as status symbols gives them actual pain. How proud I was when, a few years ago, an unpolitically correct boyfriend of mine had the following conversation with a leftie journalist friend.

LEFTIE FRIEND: Is that a Paul Smith shirt?

BOYFRIEND: Yes.

LEFTIE FRIEND: That's the same Paul Smith shirt you wore last time I met you, isn't it?

BOYFRIEND: Yes, it must be.

LEFTIE FRIEND: This skirt is by Issey Miyake.

BOYFRIEND: Really? (*Pause*) Correct me if I'm wrong, but isn't it usually aspiring gangsta rappers who set such store by designer labels?

*Leftie friend's jaw drops; end of conversation*

It has been amusing to note, of course, while writing this book, that the government has drawn up a "Respect Agenda". It will be interesting to see how they sell this optimistic document to the British people. Have you ever noticed how many role models there are in popular culture for rudeness, crassness, laddishness, and nastiness? "Ooh, Anne Robinson! She so *rude!*" "Oh, Jonathan Ross! He's so *rude!*" "Oh, Graham Norton! He's so *rude!*" "Oh, Ali G! He's so *rude!*" "Oh, Jeremy Paxman! He's so *rude!*" Count the role models for respectfulness, on the other hand, and after a couple of hours you will have to admit there is only one: Babe. That's it.

Just one small sturdy imaginary sheep-pig stands between us and total moral decay. "Excuse me," he says, gently tilting his little snout upwards. "I wonder if you'd care to follow me this way towards the hillside of enlightenment?" At which point a passer-by tragically fells him with a blow to the head with an umbrella and shouts, "You see? I told you it was him!"

# THE SIXTH GOOD REASON

# THE SIXTH GOOD REASON

## Someone Else Will Clean It Up

Theodore Dalrymple has been called "the best doctor-writer since William Carlos Williams". He recently stopped working as a psychiatrist in a hospital and prison in the Midlands. As a writer and columnist, he is noted for his savage anti-claptrappery, his unpopular but irrefutable ground-level reports of the poor and the criminal, his sublime prose, and the tremendous quality of his anecdotes. In his collection of essays *Life at the Bottom*, he quotes time and again from anti-social offenders. And time and again, he establishes – through his patients' unconscious "locutions of passivity" – that they have no concept whatever of accountability. "The beer went mad," they say. "Heroin's everywhere." "The knife went in." "Something must have made me do it."

"I have come to see the uncovering of this

dishonesty and self-deception as an essential part of my work," he writes. "When a man tells me, in explanation of his anti-social behaviour, that he is easily led, I ask him whether he was ever easily led to study mathematics or the subjunctives of French verbs." One man said that he had beaten up his pregnant girlfriend because of his low self-esteem, and was quite confused when Dalrymple suggested to him that surely the feeling of low self-esteem ought to be the result of the assault, rather than the cause of it. "My trouble came on again," said another (this man's "trouble" turned out to be breaking into churches, stealing their portable silver, then burning them down to destroy the evidence). However, nothing can surpass the conversation he had with a non-criminal patient, when he asked, "How would you describe your own character?" After thinking about it for a moment, the chap replied, "I take people as they come. I'm very non-judgemental."

Crime is not the subject of this book, thank goodness. I am depressed enough already. But the prevailing psychology of non-accountability is certainly one of the six reasons that the world seems a more rude and dangerous place. George Orwell once wrote that society has always seemed to demand a little more from human beings than it will get in practice. He may have been right. The trouble is, locating the concept of "society" isn't as easy as it once was. As for knowing what society "demands" – well, that's not easy, either. Most of us wish we didn't find graffiti and litter all over the place. We wish the pavements weren't regarded as chewing-gum repositories. We wish men wouldn't urinate in doorways and telephone boxes, sometimes in the hours of daylight. We wish skateboarders didn't come trundling like juggernauts along the pavement and expect us to jump for safety from their path. We wish cyclists didn't ignore traffic lights at pedestrian crossings. When we wish these things, we do it on behalf of "society". Yes, there is a whole lot of impotent communal *wishing* going on.

Now, obviously, we must take a zero tolerance attitude to this shocking state of affairs. It is quite proper that anti-social behaviour is being criminalised, since most of it is technically crime. But, annoyingly, I find I have a problem perching on this particular spot of moral high ground. It seems to be a bit prickly. My hat keeps getting blown off. It has started raining. Something tells me that I don't belong here. It is all very well to write "IMP" and "YES INDEED" and "ABSOLUTELY" in pencil next to sympathetic passages in erudite books and articles about our "network of dependencies" and "tissues of mobile relationships", and "bands of association and mutual commitment", but I find myself nevertheless secretly thinking, "What bands of association? Do I belong to any bands? What networks of dependencies? Am I involved in any networks? What tissues of relationships? Surely I would notice if I were caught up in some tissues?" Norbert Elias, in his book *The Society of Individuals* (1939), writes:

> The idea that in "reality" there is no such thing as a society, only a lot of individuals, says about as much as the statement that there is in "reality" no such thing as a house, only a lot of individual bricks, a heap of stones.

(Next to this passage, incidentally, I have written the word "USE".)

My problem is, you see, that I honestly don't feel like a brick in the house of society. I don't even feel like a chimney pot, a roof tile, or a glazed porch. I am self-reliance personified, a bricky brick without a trace of mortar, and my proudest contribution to society is that I don't take anything away from it. I quite fervently believe in leaving things how you found them, placing litter in the bins provided (or carrying it until you find one), and never causing another motorist to brake or swerve. In other words, I aspire to be a zero impact member of society. But does this qualify me as the opposite of an anti-social person? Quite honestly, I don't think it does, because that would be pro-social, which would involve acting on society's behalf, and I don't do that. "Nothing to do with me," I think, when I observe a sea of litter. And then I bugger off home. "That's a big job for somebody." "Someone really ought to do something about this."

Who dares to be public-spirited these days? The very term "public-spirited" is so outmoded that it actually took me a couple of days to remember it. There was a character called Martha Woodford in *The Archers* years ago who, rather eccentrically, used to dust and polish inside the telephone box on the village green and leave a little vase of flowers in it, but she is long dead; in her place, the heart of Ambridge significantly now has a webcam. I can think of only one example of a real-life person who is altruistically *pro*-social: a friend who collects the litter blowing about her street in Brighton and puts it in the bins. Evidently she has as little faith as me in the "While you're down there ..." anti-litter campaign I mentioned in the introduction. Anyway, it pains me to admit that I generally try to dissuade her from performing this selfless litter-bagging, on the grounds that:

1   It is not her responsibility, so why should she?
2   It is someone else's job, so why aren't *they* doing it?
3   It looks a bit obsessive/eccentric/Martha Woodford-ish.
4   She actually hates and resents doing it, so it makes her grumpy.
5   It makes me feel guilty and worthless.
6   As a general rule you should never volunteer for anything.
7   Ugh! That's other people's litter!

Actually, there is one other example. For his 2004 Channel 4 documentary *Where's Your ****ing*

*Manners?* the disc jockey Nihal Arthanayake discovered a small group of well-spoken young people
in London who spent their lunchtimes in the City
committing "Random Acts of Kindness", often by
feeding other people's parking meters. Of course,
ours is too cynical an age not to shudder and mutter
at such uncalled-for goody-goodiness. Some of us
did not enjoy the film *Amélie*, after all, and have never
been able to look a *crème brûlée* in the face again, let
alone listen to warm-hearted accordion music. We
are suspicious of people who do good things for no
reason. Anyone who departs from the principle of
overt self-interest is simply weird. I recently told a
story to a couple in a check-in queue, and I think the
conversation was quite instructive. The thing is, we
were queuing for the chance of extra leg-room on a
charter flight, so I explained how, at the start of a
previous holiday, I had managed to secure just one
seat with leg-room and had valiantly insisted that my
companion take it. And what do you know? During
the flight, my friend had a rotten time. Someone fell
on her. Someone else poured orange juice on her
nice suede shoes. The point of my story, of course,
was of the just-my-luck variety: you see how good

intentions can backfire? No good deed goes unpun-
ished, and so on. But the other people found quite
a different moral to my tale. "Bet you were glad you
chose the other seat!" they laughed. "Ha ha. Clever
you! Well done! Good story!"

!  #  *  !

So is it true that people who need people are the
luckiest people in the world? Mm. I suppose there
are several profound-sounding axioms thrown up
by popular culture that I consider completely inane,
and this is one of them. Here is a short list of the
worst offenders:

1   People who need people are the luckiest people
    in the world.
2   Love means never having to say you're sorry.
3   Life is like a box of chocolates. You never know
    what you're going to get.

Taking these in reverse order, life can certainly be
full of possibilities and surprises, but the analogy
between life and a box of chocolates breaks down

almost immediately because you *do* know what you're going to get with a box of chocolates, actually, if you can be bothered to consult the diagrams that are either supplied on a handy loose sheet or printed inside the lid. By rights, *Forrest Gump*'s catch line should have been, "Life is like a box of chocolates, and if you're sensible you will avoid the cracknels or anything with a bit of candied peel on top." Meanwhile, "Love means never having to say you're sorry" is the counsel of a scoundrel, to say the least. And as for people who need people – can you imagine a condition less fortunate? "I need people!" they must cry aloud at street corners. "Tough cheese!" comes the general reply. Perhaps the lyric actually means that the desperately lonely have a good winning record at the blackjack table or the race track. Perhaps croupiers are taught to spot the tell-tale signs of people-who-need-people during their basic training (sighing, weeping, yearning, etc.), and to deal to them automatically from the bottom of the deck. In poker games on Mississippi river boats, everyone scatters at the warning, "People-who-need-people boarded at Baton Rouge!" "Dang, they are the luckiest people in the whole danged world," says a chap in a fancy waistcoat, quickly scooping his chips into his hat and then putting it on his head. "Deal me out, Miss Cora! If'n you hear a splash, it's me a-swimmin' to safety."

Forgive the flight of fancy. The issue is whether we can claim to have a society any more, against which "anti-social" behaviour offends. Much as I hate to subscribe to any relativist argument, I am aware that there is a kind of paradox: that the less we engage with each other as a society, the more we are self-righteously outraged on "society's" behalf. I keep thinking about attitudes to smoking, and how they have changed during my own lifetime. Smoking in the presence of non-smokers (or in the house of a non-smoker) is now considered excessively rude, and this is only partly because of the medical evidence that shows it is also both dangerous and stupid. There is a marvellous radio monologue by Michael Frayn called "A Pleasure Shared" that sums up how a lot of people feel about second-hand smoke. The "Khhghm" noise is throat-clearing. The "thpp!" is a spit:

Do you spit? No? You don't mind if I do, though?

Khhghm ... Hold on, can you see a spittoon on the
table anywhere? Never mind. Sit down, sit down!
I can use my empty soup bowl. Khhghm – *thpp!*
My God, that's better. I've been sitting here all the
way through the first course just dying for one.

Personally, I hate smoking, and am largely safe
from it, but I have to be honest: I do remember a time
when it just didn't bother me. I grew up in a house
full of smoke; I worked in offices full of smoke;
I chose the upper deck on buses because I wanted
the view and didn't mind the smoke. I once actually
shared a desk *and a chair* with a chain smoker during
a very busy time at the office, and did not complain
except about the strain to my bottom. It's not that
I wasn't affected by smoke all this time, either. It
nearly did me in. At the age of twelve, I had to spend
the whole summer holiday in bed with respiratory
problems, and I continued to cough phlegm into
hankies until I left home aged eighteen. I had chest
X-rays and pointless antibiotics. I couldn't run the
length of a netball court without seeing stars. My
family talked darkly about Beth in *Little Women* and
sometimes actually cried at the thought of my inevitable early tubercular demise. Meanwhile they each

(four adults) lit small poisonous fires in an unventilated house between twenty and forty times a day, and had to redecorate the living room on a continuous, Forth Rail Bridge basis because of the build-up of orange nicotine tar on the ceiling.

My point is not that I was harmed by all this, and that we were all blind to the obvious. My point is that I used to accept something I truly don't accept any more: that being with other people involved a bit of compromise. When you were not alone, you suspended a portion of yourself. You became a member of a crowd. You didn't judge people by your own standards. I believe we have simply become a lot more sensitive to other people's behaviour in a climate of basic fearful alienation. Instead of a little vase of flowers inside the telephone box, there is a webcam keeping an eye on it. There was recently a news story that ostensibly proved that the world is now one big caring community, in which a webcam led to an exciting rescue: a woman in a stables in Charlotte, Iowa, was kicked by a foaling horse and was unable to move; people who had been watching her on their computers in England and Australia alerted the local rescue services and saved her life.

Now, is this heart-warming to you, or just unbeliev-ably worrying?

The breakdown of "community" has, of course, been well noted already by political scientists, both here and in America: Robert D. Putnam's powerful (and wonderfully titled) book *Bowling Alone* (2000) was a bestseller, despite the rather depressing cover illustration of an Edward Hopper-ish loner at a yellow bowling alley, with head bowed and no visible mates. Putnam sees a broad pattern that resonates in Britain as much as in America: for the first two thirds of the twentieth century, a tide bore Ameri-cans deeper into the life of their communities, but a few decades ago, the tide changed and "a treach-erous rip current" started to pull everything back. "Without at first noticing, we have been pulled apart from one another and from our communities over the last third of the century."

Some will counter-argue that they have a lot more friends these days, too many to keep up with; and may even belong to more clubs and reading groups. But Putnam distinguishes usefully between two basic types of "social capital" – *bridging* and *bonding* – to rather sobering effect. Bridging is inclusive;

bonding is exclusive. The ultimate bridging group would be the Civil Rights Movement; the ultimate bonding group would be the Ku Klux Klan. Bridging is a lubricant; bonding is an adhesive. Bridging obliges you to adapt and compromise (it generates "broader identities and reciprocity"); bonding confirms you are perfectly all right defining yourself by your existing desires and connections (it "bolsters our narrower selves"). And guess which type is doing quite well at the moment? Here's a clue: think pointy hats and flaming crosses. Think Loctite superglue. Think like-minded nutcases gratefully locating each other on the internet and secretly watching women getting kicked by horses in faraway Charlotte, Iowa.

! # * !

In the introduction to this book, I quoted Benjamin Rush from 1786, to the effect that a schoolboy should learn that "he does not belong to himself, but that he is public property". Is there any chance of a general return to the idea that the individual just owes *something* to the world around him? I have just remembered, incidentally, that in the absence of adequate street-lighting near my house, I do keep an outside light constantly burning in a spirit of general helpfulness, so maybe I am a modern saint after all. Phew. When they make lists of heroines in the future, this outside-light thing will doubtless ensure me a place alongside women who rowed lifeboats in tempests and tended the gangrenous in the Crimea. They can put it on my gravestone: "She lit the way for others." And underneath, "On the other hand, she was a shockingly bad recycler."

I tend to think in terms of bits of the brain. I once got interested in phrenology and dabbled in primitive neuro-science, and now I can't sort things out any other way. So here's how I see the present situation vis-à-vis our instinct for civic responsibility. I think we all have, hard-wired, a bit of the brain that makes a moral calculation on behalf of the common good and decides to act on it. This bit of the brain has, however, been through some tough, attenuating times recently. It has not been much called upon, and has therefore shrunk and dwindled and dried out. In fact, if I can get technical for a moment, our prevailing mode of selfishness has *sucked all the juice* out of that bit of the brain, and it is now just a tragic handful of dust, like that old sibyl in ancient times who asked Apollo for everlasting life and forgot to ask for everlasting youth – condemned to exist eternally, without hope, thirsty, in pain and loneliness and everlasting dark.

But it does still live! You see a vestige of it (oddly enough) in the way we drive: we sometimes calculate that, if we drop back a bit in the middle lane, it will allow someone in the slow lane to move out, which will allow someone else on the slip-road to join later – and no one will have to slow down and everyone will be safer and happier. In cars hurtling at 70 miles per hour, such calculations have quite a large element of self-preservation in them, admittedly; but I do uphold that they employ the bit of the brain marked "FOR THE COMMON GOOD", nevertheless. For the split second of that decision, we acknowledge that we are part of a bigger picture, and that we have a duty to improve the bigger picture if we can. We have absolutely no personal feelings about the people in the other cars. Their right to share the road with us is incontestable. They have our respect. We are all equal in the sight of the Highway Code.

According to some analysts, we can't extend this

sense of civic duty to individuals, because we feel we have to be friends with people – or at least know them – in order to be decent towards them. "Civility is not the same as affection," writes Stephen L. Carter in his book *Civility*. Richard Sennett likewise argues that the desire for some sort of intimacy in all our relationships is the enemy of civility. Our eagerness to make friends with the plumber and chat about dog tracks with the man at the booking agency is based on the idea that, once you know someone, you can respect them. But it reinforces the corollary idea: that if you *don't* know someone, you needn't have any time for them at all. Sennett, in *The Fall of Public Man* (1977), warns that we can't relate to each other as a polity until we rediscover the value of "bands of association and mutual commitment … between people who are not joined by ties of family or intimate association".

Kindness is still in the world, of course. Morality is still in the world, too. But the old connection between manners and morality has been demolished. Many people now believe that it is harmful, unhelpful and simply wrong to judge a person by the way he behaves. To demand consideration from others is to offend against a kind of modern propriety which understands that each of us has a personal morality, but is under no obligation to prove it. We regard our morality less as a guide to action or conscience, more a hidden jewel – enshrined within, inviolable, and nobody else's business. There is a line in the new *Batman* film which I can't quote exactly but is, in other words: "It's not who you are deep inside that matters, Bruce Wayne; it's what you do that defines you." Morally speaking, however, *Batman Begins* is a bit confused and should not be taken as a model for good living. For one thing, the morally squalid city of Gotham does not appear to be worth saving from obliteration; in fact, the obliteration of Gotham looks like a dandy idea. And for another, the myth of the lone superhero who swoops down and saves everybody with his bat-cunning and bat-ability may provide vicarious moral bat-pleasure (especially when he spreads his wings with a wonderful *Wump!*), but let's face it, it also lets us off the bat-hook. It is, after all, the ultimate confirmation of the view, "Someone else will clean it up."

! # \* !

What can be done? Well, ha ha, search me. All I know is that I am sick of hearing mothers tell their children, "That was a bad thing to do, Timmy, but you are not bad for doing it." I am also horrified by scenes in gritty TV dramas (presumably based on some sort of middle-class family reality beyond my own experience) where solemn, self-possessed children sit down at kitchen tables with their parents and tick them off for the rotten job they are doing. "It's time you treated us with respect, Alan," they say to their Dad. Or, "Shape up, John. Floy and I have decided you're disgusting." And the Dad hangs his head and mumbles an apology. Something seems to have gone seriously awry here. Topsy-turvy is the word. A few years ago, a friend of mine, with a difficult two-year-old, explained to me, "She didn't ask to be born, did she? Therefore I have to spend my whole life making it up to her." It took me quite a while to pin down what was odd about this statement, but I finally nailed it. It was the contrast to the old days, when the parental attitude was, "We didn't ask to have this child, did we? Therefore she had better spend her whole life making it up to us."

We all knew from the very start that this book

would end up as a moral homily. I have used every angle I could think of before reaching this point; I have even experimented with a bit of relativism, which probably didn't fool anybody. However, it is time to be plain at last. Rudeness is bad. Manners are good. It feels very daring to come out and say it, but I've done it and I feel better. I have used the words "bad" and "good", and thereby committed the ultimate political fuddy-duddiness, and doubtless undermined all my good work. Modern people are impatient with the bad–good distinction; they consider it intellectually primitive. But rudeness is a moral issue and it always has been. The way people behave towards each other, even in minor things, is a measure of their value as human beings. Henry James wrote: "Three things in human life are important. The first is to be kind. The second is to be kind. And the third is to be kind."

Ignore the small niceties and what happens? There is a splendid passage in Dickens's *Martin Chuzzlewit*, when Martin is appalled (as Dickens himself had been) by the brutish manners in 1840s America, and is told that America has better things to do than "acquire forms". He is enraged – and warns what tolerance of bad manners can lead to:

> "The mass of your countrymen begin by stubbornly neglecting little social observances, which have nothing to do with gentility, custom, usage, government, or country, but are acts of common, decent, natural, human politeness. You abet them in this, by resenting all attacks upon their social offences as if they were a beautiful national feature. From disregarding small obligations they come in course to disregard great ones; and so refuse to pay their debts. What they may do, or what they may refuse to do next, I don't know; but any man may see if he will, that it will be something following in natural succession, and a part of one great growth, which is rotten at the root."

Substitute modern relativist values for pioneering American ones, and the point is quite well made. Bad manners lead to other kinds of badness. If we each let the "FOR THE COMMON GOOD" bit of our brains shrivel on the vine, the ultimate result is crime, alienation and moral hell. Manners are easy to dismiss from discussions of morality because they seem to be trivial; the words "moral panic" were invented to belittle those of us who burst into tears at the news that 300,000 bits of chewing-gum sit, newly spat, on the pavements of Oxford Street at any one time. But if we can't talk about the morality of manners, we can't talk about the morality of anything. As Mark Caldwell puts it, in his *Short History of Rudeness*, "Manners are what is left when serious issues of human relations are removed from consideration, yet without manners serious human relations are impossible."

The problem is that it has become politically awkward to draw attention to absolutes of bad and good. In place of manners, we now have doctrines of political correctness, against which one offends at one's peril: by means of a considerable circular logic, such offences mark you as reactionary and *therefore a bad person*. Therefore if you say people are bad, *you* are bad. And to state that a well-mannered person is superior to an ill-mannered one – well, it is to invite total ignominy. Yet I can't not say this. I believe it. Manners are about showing consideration, and using empathy. But they are also about being connected to the common good; they are about being *better*. Every time a person asks himself, "What would the world be like if everyone did this?"

or "I'm not going to calculate the cost to me on this occasion. I'm just going to do the right thing", or "Someone seems to need this seat more than I do", the world becomes a better place. It is ennobled. The crying shame about modern rudeness is that it's such a terrible missed opportunity for a different kind of manners – manners based, for the first time, not on class and snobbery, but on a kind of voluntary charity that dignifies both the giver and the receiver by being a system of mutual, civil respect.

Instead of which, sadly, we have people who say, "The beer went mad" when what they mean is, "I drank too much and then I got violent." Far from taking moral responsibility for other people, we have started refusing to take moral responsibility even for ourselves. I once heard someone say, in all seriousness, "If I contract salmonella from eating this runny egg, they'll be sorry." Someone else is always the repository for blame. Someone else will clear it up. Someone else will pay for this. Even when we are offended, we don't feel comfortable saying, "This offends me." Instead, we say, "This could offend people more sensitive to this kind of thing." There was recently a hoo-ha about a TV advertisement for

Kentucky Fried Chicken in which call-centre staff sang, with their mouths full, about how great the new KFC chicken salad was – with subtitles, because their words were so unclear. Now, the Advertising Standards Authority received over a thousand complaints in two weeks, and the complaints were that:

1  It set a bad example to children.
2  It encouraged dangerous behaviour because of the risk of choking.
3  It presented emergency call-centre staff in a bad light.
4  It mocked people with speech impediments.

Evidently the true reaction, the true objection – that watching people talk with their mouths full is something you perhaps shouldn't be subjected to in your own home – simply could not be voiced, because such a point would be judgemental and therefore inadmissible.

I mentioned, in the introduction to this book, a tiny flame of hope, and here it is. Let's try *pretending* to be polite, and see what happens. Old Aristotle might have been right all those centuries ago: that if you practise being good in small things (I'm para-phrasing again), it can lead to the improvement of general morality. I promise I will stop shouting at boys on skateboards, if that will help. Being friendly and familiar with strangers is not the same as being polite (as we have seen), but if it helps us overcome our normal reticence, all right, be friendly. Yes, we live in an aggressive "Talk to the hand" world. Yes, we are systematically alienated and have no sense of community. Yes, we swear a lot more than we used to, and we prefer to be inside our own individual Bart Simpson bubbles. But just because these are the conditions that promote rudeness does not mean that we can't choose to improve our happiness by deciding to be polite to one another. Just as enough people going around correcting apostrophes may ultimately lead to some restoration of respect for the English language, so enough people demonstrating kindness and good manners may ultimately have an impact on social morality. Evelyn Waugh wrote that, historically, ceremony and etiquette were the signs of an advancing civilisation; but he went on, rather wonderfully: "They can also be the protection of [civilisations] in decline; strong defences behind

which the delicate and the valuable are preserved."
Or, if we can't go quite that far, let's just remember
to put the empty beer can in the bin *while we're down
there* ...

# Conclusion:
# Talk to the Hand

The day began quite oddly for Jim. As he started his daily ablutions, he was quite surprised to hear an interviewer on the *Today* programme say, "I'm so sorry, I didn't mean to interrupt, how rude of me to rush you, minister; do carry on." In fact, he immediately checked the date on his watch to see that it wasn't April 1. From the sports news he learned that Harry Redknapp, arriving at Portsmouth FC, had been quite hurt by some heckling and booing, but had said that he could understand where the reaction came from. "They feel betrayed and I'm sorry," said Redknapp. "I have never knowingly hurt anyone else's feelings, and I don't want to start now. People who love football have so much in common, it's a shame to be aggressive all the time. I blame the high levels of testosterone."

Jim breakfasted and then got into his car, where the oddness did not diminish. A well-groomed woman in a shiny-new sports utility vehicle not only braked to let him out of his drive, but waved a friendly "After you". This had never happened before in the history of motoring. Jim thought, "Either I have woken up in *The Truman Show* or everyone in the world got books on politeness for Christmas." At the traffic lights, a cyclist stopped alongside Jim's car and called out to the pedestrians hesitating at the kerb, "After you. Your right of way, I think!" A man making a mobile call on the street was heard to say, "I've just realised something, Jenny. Other people can hear me. Isn't that awful? I'll call you back when I'm on my own somewhere." As Jim pulled away from the lights, another car cut in front of him rather sharply, and a light flashed, "SORRY" in the back window. And then it flashed, "ARE YOU ALL RIGHT?" And then it flashed, "WHAT WOULD THE WORLD BE LIKE IF EVERYONE BEHAVED THAT WAY, EH?" And then it flashed, "HAVE YOU READ ANY ERVING GOFFMAN, BY ANY CHANCE?" As he drove down the high street, his eye was caught by a number of young people who – well, it was a bit hard to see exactly what they were doing, but they *appeared* to be collecting litter while engaged in oral sex. "This is like a dream," he said to himself. "This is very like a dream ..."

"Good morning," said the man in the coffee shop across the street from the office. "How about a regular coffee, with no poncing about?" "That would be great," said Jim, gratefully. "Excuse me," said a woman, as she reached past him for a muffin. Her child trod on his foot. "Your child just trod on my foot," said Jim. The woman looked shocked. "Did he? I'm so sorry," she said. She turned to the child and wagged her finger. "That wasn't a particularly bad thing to do, Benjamin, but you *were very bad to do it*." "Eff Off," said the child, and there was a short, universal gasp, followed by an explosion of merry laughter. "Where *did* you pick up such an outmoded expression, Benjamin?" said his mother. "Ha ha ha," they all laughed. The child ground his teeth and looked like murder, but, having no other weapons in his armoury, was forced to shut up. The till got stuck, but the coffee-shop man resourcefully used his own money to make change, so as not to hold up customers who were in a hurry. "I can fix this later when there's no one here," he explained. In a far corner, there was a small rumpus when a facetious man said, "Ooh, World-Famous Author eats toasted sandwich," and a large blonde woman punched him in the face. Jim held the door open for everyone on the way out. "Thank you," said the woman with the child. "Fwwhhhfff," said the facetious man, clutching his nose. "Eff Off," said the child, again. "Ha ha, what a funny little chap," was the general response.

At the office, Jim tried to sort out a problem with broadband and called his internet service provider helpline in Dublin. It turned out to be terribly complicated. In fact, they had been jointly wrestling with Jim's problem for a full half-hour when the operative came up with a suggestion. "Look, you can't manage this on your own, can you?" she said. "If I hop on the 12.35 to Heathrow, I can be with you in less than three hours; it's the least we can do when you've spent so much time and money on this silly problem already." Jim thought this was fair enough. He then received a call from Barclaycard. "We have noticed from your card-usage that you haven't been abroad lately. You used to travel several times a year. Please tell us it's not our fault." "Oh dear," said Jim. "Actually, it is your fault, I can't lie." "That's what we were afraid of," they said. "We feel terrible now. We may have to go off and kill ourselves." "Well, remember to list yourself under 'Various'," he offered, helpfully.

On his return home, he caught the second half of *The Weakest Link*, in which Anne Robinson was assuring a very plain female contestant, "Honestly, what terrible self-esteem some women have; it makes me despair. That's a *lovely* outfit. You really shouldn't run yourself down like that." At the end of the show, the contestants spoke warmly about the host's sense of fair play and attractive appearance. While he was at home, getting showered and changed, he had just enough time (i.e. forty-five minutes) to call and register a new credit card that had arrived in the post. "Welcome to Bastardcard," said the recorded message. "We have heard that customers find our extreme courtesy a bit unconvincing. So here's the deal. You are in a queue. Get used to being in a queue. We couldn't give a toss that you're in a queue. Get your details ready and don't try any funny stuff. Actually, I've just looked and there's no one here. Phone back if you like. Not that you have a choice, if you want to use that precious card of yours."

It occurred to Jim that he should quit while he was ahead. But he had been invited to a party that evening, and he felt he should go. As usual, when he arrived, he felt overwhelmed. He didn't know anyone, and people were always so cagey about telling you who they were. "I'm Jim," he said to the first chap he encountered. "I'm here because I do the books for the gallery. I don't suppose you'd like to disclose the mystery of your identity?" The chap shook his hand. "I'm Batman," he said. "I usually don't disclose my identity quite so readily to strangers, but I was somehow disarmed by your attractive candour." Jim realised that without the usual Twenty Questions to occupy the time, he didn't have a lot to say to Batman. Finally, he thought of something. "Er, is it true that it's what you do rather than what you are deep inside that defines you?" Batman thought about it. "I can see where you're coming from with that, Jim," he said. "But to be honest, I'm in it mainly for the fetishy body armour and the flying."

It was on the return journey that the oddness of the day began, tragically, to wear off. A young woman in the taxi queue was saying into her mobile phone, "Yeah, well, like, talk to the hand coz the face ain't listening." Jim winced. Oh no, he thought; it can't be happening. Someone with Eff Off tattooed on his forehead (back-to-front) spat chewing gum onto Jim's shoes and then glared at him. In the taxi, the radio was tuned, very loudly, to Radio Git FM, and the driver didn't say hello. At home, several messages were waiting on his answering machine. One was from British Gas to tell him that, *for less than the price of a Mars bar*, he could phone back between the hours of 8am and 5pm and find out what their latest utterly annoying offer was. Another was from Barclaycard to say that it was now a condition of holding the card that you travelled abroad at least three times a year, so his account had been cancelled. When Jim switched on the TV, he found a choice of: (1) Jonathan Ross being cheeky to someone famous, (2) Jeremy Paxman being rude to someone important, (3) a houseful of so-called "celebrities" cutting each other down to size, and (4) a game show in which contestants were allowed to torture and humiliate the judges, to the baying and jeering of a drunken teenage audience.

He went to bed. He lay still for a few minutes, mulling over the day's events. "I wonder if the issue of rudeness is a very big important one, or a very small silly one," he said to himself, at last. "All I know is that since I read Lynne Truss's *Talk to the Hand*, I seem to be all the more confused." He drifted off to sleep, and there we will leave him. Poor sod. He'd been hoping for a list of rules, and what he'd got instead were six lessons in heightened sensitivity and existential horror. "How *do* you collect litter while engaging in oral sex?" was his last conscious thought. He was not alone in wondering that, of course. Why don't we all write to Keep Britain Tidy and ask them what on earth was on their minds?

# Bibliography

Allan Bloom, *The Closing of the American Mind*, Simon
    and Schuster, 1987
P. Brown and S.C. Levinson, *Politeness: Some
    Universals in Language Usage*, Cambridge
    University Press, 1987
Mark Caldwell, *A Short History of Rudeness: Manners,
    Morals and Misbehavior in Modern America*, Picador
    USA, 1999
Stephen L. Carter, *Civility: Manners, Morals, and the
    Etiquette of Democracy*, 1998
Theodore Dalrymple, *Life at the Bottom: The Worldview
    That Makes the Underclass*, Ivan R. Dee, 2001
Barbara Ehrenreich, "The Civility Glut", *The
    Progressive*, vol. 64, issue 12, December 2000

Norbert Elias, *The Civilizing Process: Sociogenetic and Psychogenetic Investigations* (1939), Blackwell, 1994; rev. edn 2000

Norbert Elias, *The Society of Individuals* (1983), Blackwell, 1991

Kate Fox, *Watching the English: The Hidden Rules of English Behaviour*, Hodder and Stoughton Ltd, 2004

Michael Frayn, "A Pleasure Shared", from *Listen to This: Sketches and Monologues*, Methuen, 1990

Erving Goffman, *Behavior in Public Places: Notes on the Social Organization of Gatherings*, Free Press, 1963

Erving Goffman, *Interaction Ritual: Essays on Face-to-Face Behavior*, Pantheon, 1967 (Aldine Transaction, 2005)

Erving Goffman, *The Presentation of Self in Everyday Life*, Anchor Books, 1959 (Penguin, 2005)

Erving Goffman, *Relations in Public: Microstudies of the Public Order*, Allen Lane, 1971

Robert Hughes, *Culture of Complaint: The Fraying of America*, Oxford University Press USA, 1993 (Harvill Press, 1994)

Steven Johnson, *Everything Bad is Good for You*, Allen Lane, 2005

Richard Layard, Happiness: Lessons from a New Science, Allen Lane, 2005

Carolyn Marvin, When Old Technologies were New: Thinking about Electric Communication in the Late Nineteenth Century, Oxford University Press USA, 1988

George Mikes, How to be a Brit, André Deutsch, 1984 (Penguin, 1986)

John Morgan, Debrett's New Guide to Etiquette and Modern Manners, Headline, 1999

Jeremy Paxman, The English: A Portrait of a People, Michael Joseph, 1998 (Penguin 1999)

Stuart Prebble, Grumpy Old Men, BBC, 2004

Public Agenda, Aggravating Circumstances: A Status Report on Rudeness in America, 2002

Robert D. Putnam, Bowling Alone: The Collapse and Revival of American Community, Simon and Schuster, 2000

John Seabrook, Deeper: A Two-Year Odyssey in Cyberspace, Faber and Faber, 1997

Richard Sennett, The Fall of Public Man, Knopf, 1977 (Penguin, 2003)

Richard Sennett, Respect in a World of Inequality, W. W. Norton, 2003 (Penguin, 2004)

Evelyn Waugh, "Manners and Morals", from *The Essays, Articles and Reviews of Evelyn Waugh*, ed. Donat Gallagher, Methuen, 1984